Healing Waters, Tranquil Valleys
Bath County, Virginia

by

Anne Drake McClung

with photography by

Ellen M. Martin

and

Anne Drake McClung

production, layout, and illustration by Arthur M. Lipscomb III, Alone Mill Media

Alone Mill Publishing

Library of Congress Catalog Number: 2004112929

ISBN: 0-9675205-2-5

Printed in China through Asia Pacific Offset, Inc.

Acknowledgements

On each of the many, many visits to Bath to research, to explore, or to photograph, we were struck by the kindness of Bath's residents. Wherever we went, our interactions with folks were always fun, satisfying, and helpful. Thank you all for your help.

A very warm and special thanks to Barbara Ringer and Mary Lyle. Their contributions in support and editing have been enormous and their energy boundless as they helped us through this project.

There were also many individuals and businesses that went out of their way to show us, lead us, or provide to us wonderful old photographs. The individuals were Hugh Gwin, Laurence Brunson, Richard Armstrong, Margo Oxendine, Joe and Kathy Wood, Paul Howell, Emmie Hicklin, Debi Ratliff, Evelyn Grau, Pat Davenport, Mr. and Mrs. Paul Lancaster, and Phebe Cambata. Crucial resources were the Bath County Historical Society, The Homestead, the Bath County Library, the Library of Virginia, and BARC. Thank you.

And finally, I want to thank my father, Fran Drake, and his colleague and our family friend, Marshall Fishwick, for their devotion and support. You gentlemen are the best.

Preface

In this fascinating, carefully crafted book we get a new look at old Bath County, one of the gems in Virginia's crown. Indeed, there are few places in America, or the world, that can match its unique combination of mountains, vistas, history, springs, and spas. Where else might one find an unspoiled Cowpasture River with a tributary called the Bullpasture? Or healing waters such as Warm Springs, where for over two centuries have attracted thousands to 'take the waters,' constant at 98 degrees, where the 1761 bath house encloses 60,000 gallons of water in a pool? No wonder the aging Thomas Jefferson came by coach from Monticello to help cure his ills. Five miles down the Warm Springs Valley is The Homestead, one of America's finest resort hotels, with some of the best golf courses and cuisine in the country.

Both the prose and visuals (many aerial views) are breathtaking. Having spent years writing books about the Old Dominion, including *Springlore In Virginia*, I know that true places are reached not by roads but by insights. As history and art, this book is a treasure. If only we can keep Bath County like this! If only we can get Anne McClung and colleagues to do more books that are as important as this one!

Marshall W. Fishwick

Table of Contents

Bath: An Introduction

The Commonwealth of Virginia can boast of counties that are charmingly rustic, counties that are resplendent with mountains and valleys, counties that are well-watered with rivers and springs, but Bath County is unique. It combines all these features, and a good deal more, in a single region. Unspoiled and little known to the world at large, Bath is certainly one of Virginia's most beautiful counties.

Aerial view of Griffith Knob located near the Bath/Alleghany border.

Bath County is located in the west central area of Virginia, with its western-most border at the Virginia/West Virginia line. In West Virginia its neighboring counties are Pocahontas and Greenbrier. The Virginia counties neighboring it are Highland ("Little Switzerland") to the north, Alleghany to the south, and Augusta and Rockbridge to the east. Bath's boundaries contain 540 square miles (345,000 acres). On the map the county seems to take the shape of a slightly tilted quadrangle with four distinct corners pointing east toward the Shenandoah Valley, north toward Morgan-town, West Virginia, south toward Roanoke and south-ern Virginia, and west toward Charleston, West Virginia.

In comparison with most other Virginia counties, Bath's population of about 5000 is mi-nuscule. The highest population density is concentrated in two areas: the Warm Springs Valley, which includes Warm Springs and Hot Springs, and the eastern part of the county around the com-munities of Millboro and Millboro Springs. The county includes about twelve small communities but not a single incorporated

This greyscale image is the combination of 16 adjoining elevation data sets obtained from the USGS website and which cover the area in which Bath County rests. Elevation data is related to the greyscale value of a pixel to produce the image at right. The greyscale value can then be used to extrude a terrain in modeling software where lights can be set to generate the terrain shadows seen on the next page.

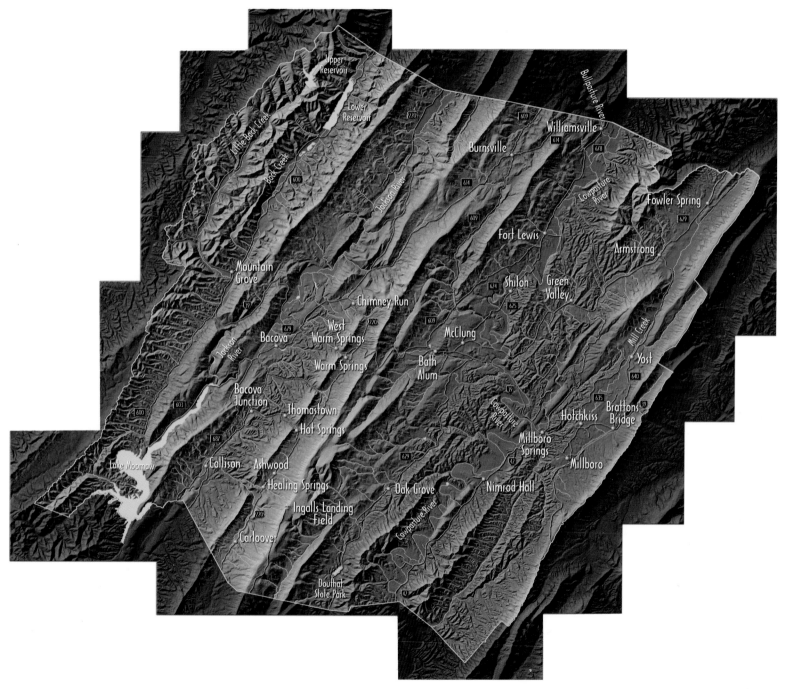

Upper Reservoir

Lower Reservoir

Bullpasture River

Little Back Creek

Back Creek

Jackson River

220

609

Williamsville

614

678

Burnsville

Cowpasture River

Fowler Spring

629

600

Fort Lewis

Armstrong

609

Mountain Grove

624 Shiloh

Green Valley

39

625

Mill Creek

Chimney Run

Jackson River

679

West Warm Springs

220

609

McClung

Yost

Bacova

640

Warm Springs

Bath Alum

635

Bacova Junction

39

Cowpasture River

Hotchkiss

Brattons Bridge

600

603

Thomastown

39

Hot Springs

Millboro Springs

687

629

Millboro

Lake Moomaw

Callison

Ashwood

42

Healing Springs

Oak Grove

Nimrod Hall

220

Ingalls Landing Field

Cowpasture River

Carloover

Douthat State Park

42

town. And, as astonishing as it may seem, there are no traffic lights anywhere in Bath County!

The whole of Bath County lies at a relatively high elevation. Its highest elevation of 4,477 feet is found on the western border, known as the Allegheny Front, atop Paddy's Knob. The lowest point in the county is 1,140 feet at a location in the southeastern part of the county along the Cowpasture River.

A wintry scene with a lone blackbird taken near Hot Springs.

The mountains of Bath County are all part of the Allegheny chain, which runs south from western Pennsylvania into Virginia and West Virginia. The Alleghenies are part of the Appalachian Mountains, which run from the Gaspe Peninsula in eastern Quebec, Canada, all the way south to Alabama. It is no exaggeration to say that the Allegheny Mountains in Bath County, Virginia, make up some of the most breathtakingly beautiful ranges of the entire Appalachian chain.

Aerial view of Douthat State Park Lake.

Indeed, the mountains seem to rise and fall endlessly like a green ocean across the entire county. Of the 345,000 acres in Bath, an astounding 89% is in forest. Over one half of this acreage comprises the George Washington Na-

Aerial view taken from Bath looking south toward Covington. The smoke billowing from the smoke stacks of Westvaco can be seen in the distance.

tional Forest. Some 4% or 13,428 acres make up the T. M. Gathright Wildlife Management Area, which is managed by the Virginia Commission Of Game And Inland Fisheries. Voluntary protection on private lands includes seventeen

Aerial view of mountains and more mountains.

conservation easements which encompass 8,716 acres. Another 9,000 acres on Warm Springs Mountain was sold by the Hot Springs, Inc. to the Nature Conservancy. This particular acreage is one of the largest and most ecologically important tracts of privately owned forest in Virginia. According to the Nature Conservancy, the area includes a globally rare montane pine barren and an old-growth hickory forest, which provide habitat for several rare plants and invertebrates.

Aerial view of Lake Moomaw and the seemingly endless ridges of mountains.

Each small community within Bath County is unique, and there is much to see in every one of them. Foremost, of course, is The Homestead in Hot Springs. Dating from 1766, it is a majestic, nationally and internationally known resort hotel which offers access to the sublime warm and hot springs in Bath County, world class golf courses, the finest cuisine imaginable, and accommodations fit for royalty and commoners alike. Bath is also home to several splendid facilities for camping and outdoor recreation aimed at those wanting to spend time with nature. Douthat State Park, built by the Civilian Conservation Corps in the 1930s, boasts a beautiful mountain lake, rental cabins and camping facilities, boating, swim-

ming, fishing, and hiking. Douthat provides a perfect place for a temporary escape from the cares of city living.

Another man-made lake, this one larger and higher in the western mountains of the county, is Lake Moomaw, which offers all of the amenities a nature lover could desire. Visitors to Lake Moomaw feel they are in another world where one couldn't possibly imagine anything but peace and quiet and where, in many places, there is not a hint of modern civilization.

The forest floor atop Warm Springs Mountain.

In contrast, Bath County is also home to a product of the modern age: the world's largest pumped storage station which supplies elec-

tricity to six states. But in recognition of the ecological importance of the natural region from which it was carved, the station also provides a nearby lake for recreational activities.

There are two major rivers that run north to south the length of Bath County: the Jackson and the Cowpasture. Both rivers flow into Bath from neighboring Highland County and, according to geologists, these rivers traversing this 'valley and ridge country' have existed since the Paleozoic era millions of years ago.

The Cowpasture has a tributary called the Bullpasture, which joins it in the northern part of the county. There are also a number of large creeks in Bath that join the two main streams and that contribute to the county's reputation for being one of the best-watered regions in the state. The courses of the Cowpasture and the Jackson are almost parallel, with the Jackson on the western side and the Cowpasture more eastward. The Jackson River is

A scene on the Cowpasture River near Nimrod Hall.

named for William Jackson, one of the early settlers who claimed land along the river.

The Cowpasture is an exceptionally clean river, and controversies have continually swirled around the issue of how best to keep it so. According to Deane and Garvey Winegar in their *Highroad Guide to the Virginia Mountains:* "So clean is the water of the Cowpasture that a bluegill or watersnake casts a shadow against the smooth rock bottom even in deep pools. The river's clarity makes it a pleasure to wade, swim, fish, or just to watch

A similar scene on the Jackson River at Hidden Valley.

aquatic life." The Cowpasture once watered rich hunting grounds frequented by the Shawnees, who are said to have called it the Wallawhatoola. There are several interpretations of the word's meaning in the Shawnee language, but the most curious and quite believable version came from a Millboro physician of long ago, Dr. Samuel Hileman,

View of the valley taken from atop Warm Springs Mountain near Ingalls Landing Field.

who thought it meant "figure drawn on the ground as the walking bull buffalo urinates."

As it is with virtually all settlements throughout the world, the natural configuration of mountains, valleys, and streams dictates where homesteaders homestead and settlements develop. Humans often believe that they have complete control of their lives but in reality, at least in our mountainous regions, our lives have always been shaped and determined by the relationship we have with the unique arrangements of the mountains and the valley floor. The story of the earliest European settlements in Bath County follows the same pattern as that of the settlements in neighboring counties, particularly Rockbridge and Augusta. In every case the colonial governor of Virginia was petitioned by individuals to be given land grants from the English Crown. In Bath County individuals asked for a 50,000 acre grant on the head branches of the James River as early as 1727 and permanent settlers eventually staked out their claims along the Cowpasture and the Jackson Rivers around 1744.

By the mid 1700s the Lewis family, true pioneers in the history of western Virginia, had already either settled in, or surveyed, the Beverley Land Grant around Staunton, Virginia, and the Borden Land Grant in neighboring Rockbridge County. Thomas and Andrew Lewis conducted the first land surveys for Bath County and also claimed much land for themselves.

In Oren Morton's *Annals of Bath County*, he explains that there were about fourteen separately distinguishable settlements. The names of these pioneer communities, together with their approximate locations and alphabetical lists of the surnames of at least some of the settlers associated with them, are shown graphically in this chapter. Many of these names have come down through the generations and still resonate in Bath County.

During the pioneer years in Bath County the greatest impediment to settlement and the worst danger to settlers came from Native Americans. Even though Indians did not have permanent dwelling places in the region, they found it to be prime hunting ground and were determined to oppose the intrusion of European settlers. Homesteaders were constantly under the threat of Indian attacks.

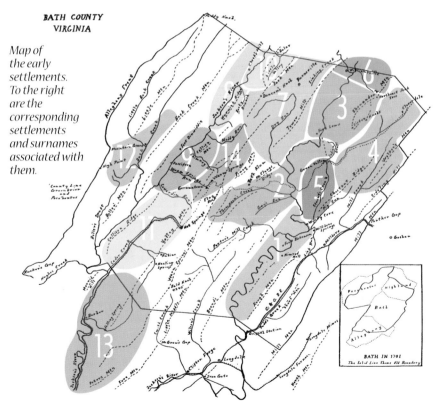

Map of the early settlements. To the right are the corresponding settlements and surnames associated with them.

In 1754, some ten years after the first settlers came to the area, the French and Indian War began. This was the last North American phase of the global conflict known at the Seven Years War. On this side of the Atlantic, the conflict was between Britain and France, together with its American Indian allies, and the stakes were very high: which of the two colonial powers would ultimately control the North American continent.

As noted by historians, Bath County played a role in these crucial hostilities and was considered a "strategic frontier for the protection of the Shenandoah Valley." George Washington was named the commander of the Virginia Militia and it is here in this strategically located Bath County that a number of forts were

1   The Dickenson Settlement

Location: Extending along the Cowpasture well below Fort Lewis into the bend at Griffith Knob.

Surnames: Abercrombie, Beard, Clendennin, Coffey, Crockett, Daugherty, Dickenson, Donally, Douglass, Gay, Gillispie, Graham, Hicklin, Insminger, Kelso, Kincaid, Lavery, Madison, Mayse, McCay, McClung, McDonald, Millroy, Mitchell, Muldock, O'Hara, Porter, Ramsey, Scott, Simpson, vSitlington, Sloan, Stuart, Thompson, Waddell, Walker, Watson.

2   The Fort Lewis Settlement

Location: Includes the Thompson Creek area and extending up the Cowpasture.

Surnames: Benson, Black, Cartmill, Cowardin, Dickey, Feamstser, Franciso, Frame, Hall, Hughart, Jackson, Knox, Lewis, Mayse, McCreery, Miller, Montgomery, Moody, Moore, Wallace.

3   The Upper-Cowpasture Settlement

Location: Included the bottomland on the Cowpasture around Laurel Gap.

Surnames: Devericks, Erwin, Gwin, Johns, Shaw, Steuart.

4   The Upper Mill Creek Settlement

Location: The basin of Mill Creek above Panther Gap.

Surnames: Bratton, Lyle, McDonald, Putnam, Rhea, Swearingen.

5   The Green Valley Settlement

Location: The upper basin of Stuart's Creek.

Surnames: Bell, Crawford, Eddy, Hall, Hepler, Fitzpatrick, McCausland, Morrow, Rucker, Warrick.

6   The Bullpature Settlement

Location: Along the course of the Bullpasture.

Surnames: Beathe, Black, Bodkin, Bradshaw, Burnside, Carlile, Curry, Davis, Duffield, Erwin, Estill, Ferguson, Graham, Harper, Hempenstall, Hicklin, Hiner, Hynes, Jones, Justice, Lockridge, Malcom, McCoy, Peebles, Pullin, Siron, Summers, Wiley.

7   The Red Holes or Burnsville Settlement

Location: Adjacent to the Bullpasture valley.

Surnames: Burns, Frame, Monroe, Williams.

8   The Wilson Settlement

Location: The northernmost 'pocket' of bottomland along the Jackson River.

Surnames: Bratton, Cleek, Given, Gwin, McFarland, Wilson

9   The Fort Dinwiddie Settlement

Location: Below the Wilson Settlement on the Jackson.

Surnames: Bourland, Byrd, Cameron, Davis, Dean, Jackson, McClintic.

10   The Little Valley Settlement

Location: East of the Wilson Settlement.

Surnames: Carpenter, McAvoy, Pritt.

11   The Fort Mann Settlement

Location: Below the Fort Dinwiddie Settlement extending up the valley of Cedar Creek.

Surnames: Armstrong, Bollar, Elliot, Kincaid, Kirk, Mann, McGuffin, Montgomery, Morris, Robinson, Walker, Wood.

12   The Vance or Mountain Grove Settlement

Location: Back Creek and Little Back Creek.

Surnames: Baxter, Gregory, Hamilton, Kelly, Vance.

13   The Potts Creek Settlment

Location: Lower course of Potts Creek.

Surnames: Potts, Persinger

14   The Warm Springs Settlement

Around Warm Springs.

Surnames: Accroding to Oren Morton there are no names of permanent settlers in this area of thermal springs as it was mainly occupied by non-residents.

Key to the map on the left of the settlements and the surnames associated with them.

built under his command. The two most prominent of these were Fort Dickinson on the Cowpasture River and Fort Dinwiddie at Hidden Valley near the Jackson River.

On his journeys to Bath County to check on the forts, Washington met a man named Thomas Bullett, who had been trained as a surveyor by the College of William And Mary, and who would become crucial in the development of The Homestead. In 1756 Washington had placed Lt. Bullett in command of Fort Dinwiddie. It was at this time that Bullett became friends with Thomas and Andrew Lewis. They knew the area well and recognized the valuable medicinal properties of the various springs in the area as well as the great potential for development where guests could be enticed to come to vacation and 'take the waters'. In June of 1763, the three friends signed an agreement to develop the Hot Springs into what became a spa resort. They obtained a land grant of three hundred acres that included all seven of the mineral springs in Hot Springs.

The French and Indian War lasted for several years and was marked by fierce fighting between militia units made up of colonial settlers under British command and various

Wild ferns found at the Cascades.

confederations of American Indian tribes. The war ended with the Treaty of Paris in 1763. However, relations with the Indians remained tense. The forts established under Washington were later kept on a stand- by status when the American Revolutionary War began but little activity was experienced in Bath County. By the time Bath County was officially organized in 1790, the Indian was only a memory.

The rich valley pastures were ideal for agriculture, which became and remained, for many generations the predominant occupation of the settlers in the region. Getting crops to market was a problem in such a remote area but several sources indicate that farmers used the county's two rivers to transport goods for short distances.

As elsewhere throughout Appalachia, a household activity that later became an industry was the distilling of whiskey. Farmers had a ready supply of corn, rye and barley and stills were not uncommon. One story, told in *The Bicentennial History of Bath County,* is not confirmed but is highly likely to have happened because it is documented that this type of thing went on in neighboring counties. It tells "…of a resourceful farmer on the Cowpasture who each winter built a large log raft. When the early spring freshets arrived he would load his annual production of corn whiskey onto the raft, strap the barrels down, and then commence floating and poling his way to Richmond. After selling his whiskey and logs the farmer proceeded to buy a wagon, a team of good horses, and all the supplies he and his neighbors would need for the coming year. Loading his provisions into the new wagon the farmer returned

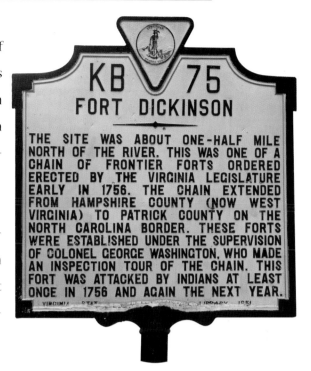

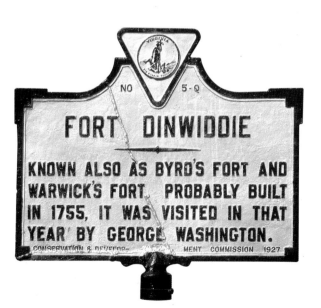

leisurely to Bath County over land."

Bath already had a rich history before it was officially recognized as a county on December 14, 1790. It was carved from the counties of Augusta, Botetourt, and Greenbrier. Originally the county of Bath was three times as large as it is today. During its first fifty years as an established county, it was reduced to smaller boundaries on several occa-

The crown of one of the largest sycamore trees in the county as listed in Virginia's Big Tree Database. The tree is along the Cowpasture.

sions. The first took place in 1796 when a three mile strip was annexed to Pendleton, West Virginia. The second reduction came in 1832 when the counties of Allegheny in Virginia and Pocahontas in West Virginia were established. And the third time, later in the 1830s, was when Pendleton and Bath were reduced to make room for Highland County.

The remaining chapters in this book will be devoted to describing and illustrating some of the main things that make Bath County so special, including its natural wonders, its man-made features, and especially its people. It is beyond the scope of this book to give every detail of the county's history and present-

The base of the large sycamore. It measures approximately 330 inches in circumference at 4 feet off the ground.

day characteristics, but a dip into at least a few of the fine works listed in the bibliography can provide the reader with more information. Most important is the hope that reading this text and viewing the photographs will lead you to explore beautiful Bath County, an experience guaranteed to be unforgettable.

Trillium on Indian Draft Road

THE SPRINGS

How remarkable it is that our Founding Father and third President, Thomas Jefferson, has left us meticulous and vivid descriptions of many of Virginia's wondrous places as they existed in the late Eighteenth Century. One can find these invaluable comments in his *Notes of the State of Virginia*, which were published in 1787, and what he had to say about The Hot and The Warm Springs is worth quoting at length:

"The springs rise near the foot of the ridge of mountains, generally called the Warm spring mountain, but on the maps Jackson's mountains. The one is distinguished by the name of the Warm spring, and the other of the Hot spring. The Warm spring issues with a very bold stream, sufficient to work a gristmill, and to keep the waters of its basin, which is 30 feet in diameter, at the vital warmth, viz. 96 degrees Fahrenheit. The matter with which these waters is allied is very volatile; its smell indicates it to be sulphurous, as also does the circumstance of its turning silver black. They relieve rheumatisms. Other complaints also of different natures have been removed or lessened. It rains here four or five days every week.

*Jordan Run at
Bath Alum Springs.*

"The Hot spring is six miles from the warm, and has been so hot as to have boiled an egg. It rises the mercury to 112 degrees, which is fever heat, and sometimes relieves where the Warm spring fails. A fountain of common water, issuing within a few inches of its margin, gives it a singular appearance. ...These springs are much resorted to in spite of a total want of accommodation for the sick. Their waters are strongest in the hottest months, which occasions their being visited in July and August principally."

Marshall Fishwick, author of *Springlore in Virginia*, and many other books, once said that people live by the mythology of their time. He said that every age is credulous in its own way and as time passes, new myths arise, which

A view of the inside of the women's pool at Warm Springs. The warm water is four feet deep and yet crystal clear.

use imagery to express the eternal in terms of the temporal. These myths end up in our hearts and minds as 'the truth.' And finally he contends that true places are reached not by roads but insights and convictions. Mythology is transformed into history; history into folklore; folklore into literature. Indian folklore is a good example of this notion. We often like to remember things and create our past in a romanticized way and pass these memories down through the generations.

As is true with most of our country's development, and is true of Bath County, there have always existed wonderful Indian legends that are carried down from generation to generation to tell of the past. If you closed your eyes and tried to imagine Bath County with no hint or form of civilization, what would you see in your mind's eye? You would see ridge after ridge of mountains. You would see narrow, lush, green valleys with plentiful fresh waters running among them. You can imagine the coming of native Americans into the area and their 'taking the waters' not so long ago in our history. Before the towns of Hot Springs and Warm Springs were developed, and even before the first European settlers began homesteading in this area, the wondrous springs in Bath County had surely been discovered.

There is an enduring legend of who first discovered the springs that speaks of an

Cascades at Healing Springs.

Indian brave in the 1600s who traveled to a sacred meeting ground for a tribunal conference. The story that is told in Fay Ingalls' *The Valley Road* tells of the young Appalachian Leopard who, in his travels to a tribunal council, comes across a pool that runs clear and warm. A night's soak in these waters revived his disheartened spirit and aching body and spurred him on tirelessly to the council. "So renewed he was by the springs that there was no one of them all was found more graceful in address, more commanding in manner, more pleasing in look, and sagacious in policy, than the young Appalachian Leopard who bathed in the 'Spring of Strength'."

The young Appalachian Leopard's account of the spring spread among the tribes. Ever since, men and women have come from all over the world to 'take the waters', if not exactly to gain extraordinary powers, but to relax and heal themselves from the emotional and physical stresses of life.

For most of the 1800s and even into the early years of the 1900s, the springs of Virginia were extremely fashionable. They were in vogue with the high society of the time and with others whose financial resources allowed

The outdoor foot spring at The Homestead.

an expensive summer tour of going from one spring to another. The Hot and Warm Springs were where much of genteel America converged for the social scene.

There was another group of people who frequented the springs throughout this period: invalids and people seeking cures for orthopedic problems and other maladies. The custom of bathing in mineral springs and drinking water from them for medicinal purposes had been an established tradition in Europe for centuries, and there was, and is, a world-famous spa in Bath, England, which was first developed by the Romans. It is easy to assume that Bath County, Virginia (as well as Berkeley Springs, now in West Virginia and officially named "Bath") took their name from the wondrous English spring. This may be true, but the Oxford English Dictionary includes a general, though now obsolete, definition of "bath" that would appropriately characterize the thermal waters of Bath County: "A spring of water (chiefly hot or impregnated with minerals) suitable for bathing."

1890 ad in Harper's Magazine.

Keeping in mind the romantic Indian legend concerning discovery of the springs, we must now look more realistically at how they were after Europeans started coming to them. In the old days a visit to the springs was no picnic. In the words of Donald Haynes of the Virginia Historical Society: "If one were truly ill, the hardships of the journey sometimes proved fatal. If one survived the trip, the primitive, unsanitary conditions

one found on arrival could bring on a relapse - - or worse, put a period to all suffering." No finger has been pointed at any one spring in particular, but contemporaneous accounts make clear that, in general, the accommodations were considerably less than pleasing. A visitor had to expect unpalatable meals, biting insects, and the groaning of the ill mingled with the nightly uproar of drinking and gambling. Despite all of this, guests must have found enough in the thermal waters, the mountain scenery, the clean air, and the companionship of other spa-goers to come back year after year wanting more.

Back in the 1980s, The Virginia Historical Society published a manuscript diary that had been kept by a Virginian during his trip to and from the springs of Virginia in 1804. Below is a segment of his account of the Warm and the Hot springs visits.

A picture of an invalid in his chair at Hot Springs. Bath County Historical Society.

"...We made a small stop at McClung's, just over the Cow pasture River, after which we cross'd the Mountain and arrived about midday at the Warm Springs, where we bathed and dressed, and after a very indifferent dinner, went in the evening to the Hot springs about five miles distant. The bath at the Warm springs is most luxurious. It is inclosed with an octangular wall; about ten yards across and in the center about 5 feet 6 inches deep, shallower at the sides. I experienced a very disagreeable sensation in coming out of the bath, the pressure of the atmosphere is great indeed, and to me very oppressive. I must have remained in half an hour. Had I been more accustomed to

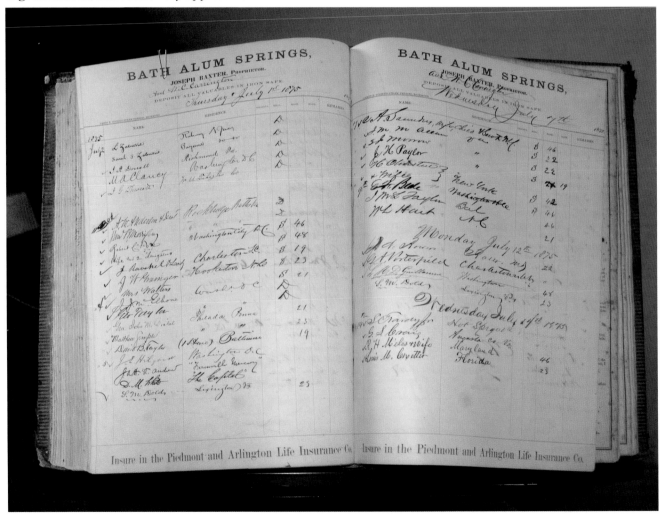

Ledger from Bath Alum Springs opened to the pages of entries of July 1, 1875 and July 7, 1875. The Cambata collection.

it, or remained a shorter Time in the bath, I possibly might not have experienced the unpleasant sensations I did. Here, tho there was very little company owing to the badness of the accommodations. ...At Hot springs we found a great deal of company, and with some difficulty procured lodging. We had intended to spend a day or two here but the sulphur spring, being the place of our destination, we became proportionable anxious, as we more nearly approached. ...tho' there was a great deal of genteel Company here of both sexes, yet I left this place, with great pleasure - for the number of invalids, afflicted with various diseases, with limbs distorted in pain, and unable to assist themselves, who were here in hopes of relief, or a mitigation of their torments, rendered an abode here, very unpleasant, to a man of feeling, unaccustomed to such scenes. After an excellent dinner, & a glass of wine, for this house is most excellently kept by Mr. Thompson, and a very amiable and notable wife, we proceeded..."

Room key to Room 24 at the old Bath Alum. The Cambata collection.

Bath Alum. Lithograph published in John J. Moorman, M.D., "The Virginia Springs," 1857.

ANALYSIS OF SULPHUR WATER

Sulphur, Wallawhatoola Alum, Chalybeate, Freestone and Alkaline Mineral.

ANALYSIS OF SULPHUR WATER.

Per U. S. Gallon of 231 Cubic Inches.

Hydrosulphate of Sodium	3.341	Grains
Sulphate of Lime	1.554	"
Sulphate of Potassium	0.105	"
Bicarbonate of Sodium	4.267	"
Bicarbonate of Magnesia	1.648	"
Bicarbonate of Lime	0.537	"
Bicarbonate of Iron	Distinct trace.	
Alumina	0.262	Grains.
Silicate of Sodium	0.885	"
Chloride of Sodium	0.466	"
Phosphate of Aluminum	Trace.	
Organic Matter	0.350	"

DISSOLVED GASES

Sulphuretted Hydrogen	1.082	Cu. Ins.
Carbon Dioxide (besides that in Bicarbonates)	6.945	" "

November 12, 1891. G. B. M. ZERR, Analyst.

Water analysis as found in the Millboro Springs College Catalog.

Brass sign from Bath Alum Springs. The Cambata collection.

Even allowing for the mixed feelings of the diarist, and assuming that other regular guests in the Warm Springs Valley found more to their liking, this sketch may serve to remind us that the "good old days" in Bath County had some features that were downright unpleasant.

The county is blessed with unique geological features providing it with an unusually large number of mineral springs. Each grouping of springs, depending on its location, is different from the others in temperature and mineral analysis. On the eastern side of Warm Springs Mountain the mineral springs of the Cowpasture are probably the coolest in the county.

The Millboro area is home to four springs of significance. The one that perhaps flourished the most during the 1700s and 1800s was Bath Alum Springs near what is now Route 39, between Millboro Springs and Warm Springs Mountain. During the many years when the only road into Bath County was from Staunton in Augusta County, historic Bath Alum was situated on this much-traveled route. It dates from about 1740 when the first pioneers began settling the area. In the mid 1800s, when the railroad established a stop in Millboro, passengers would often go on from there to Bath Alum by carriage, staying there for a few days before proceeding over the mountain to the Warm Springs. Patronage at Bath Alum included some of the greatest names in our history: Presidents Washington, Jefferson, Madison and Monroe often stayed there, and Generals Robert E. Lee and Stonewall Jackson were also frequent visitors. During the Civil

War the Bath County Troops were quartered at Bath Alum. Today, little remains of the resort and the property is privately owned.

The other three noteworthy springs on the east side of Bath County are the Millboro Springs, All Healing Springs, and the Wallawhatoola Springs. Today these springs are also privately owned and no longer used as spas by the public. However, long ago, when they were in use, the proprietors had the particular springs analyzed so they could promote the springs as a way to help heal various ailments.

Millboro Springs (Wallawhatoola) From the Beers, F. W. Illustrated Atlas of City of Richmond. 1876. Library of Virginia.

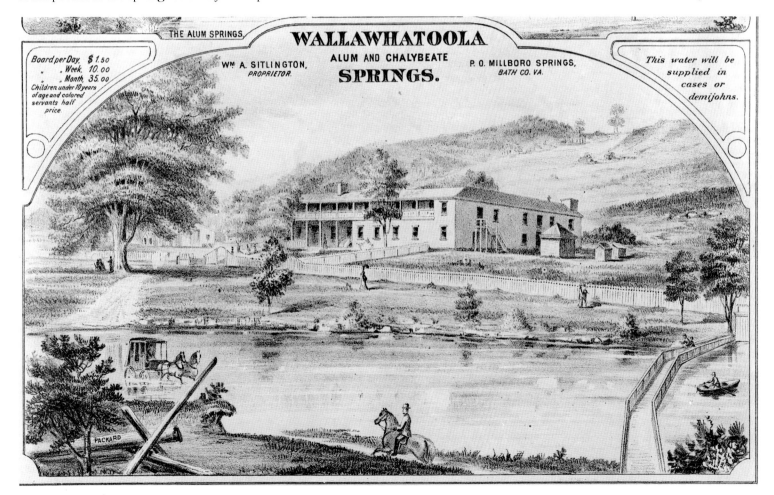

THE ALUM SPRINGS.

WALLAWHATOOLA
ALUM AND CHALYBEATE
SPRINGS.

Board per Day, $1.50
" " Week, 10.00
" " Month, 35.00
Children under 10 years of age and colored servants half price.

WM. A. SITLINGTON, PROPRIETOR.

P. O. MILLBORO SPRINGS, BATH CO. VA.

This water will be supplied in cases or demijohns.

PACKARD

On the western side of the mountains in Bath are springs whose temperatures are much warmer, some even higher than a human's normal body temperature of 98.6 degrees. There is a simple geological answer to what makes these springs so hot. When surface waters sink to very great depths and come within the influence of the earth's internal heat, they reappear with much higher temperatures than found in ordinary springs. Furthermore, since the water is so warm it absorbs an abundance of minerals from its rocky path to the surface, and this process tends further to increase the heat of the water. So, the deeper the water seeps into the earth, the warmer it will be when it reappears. In geologists' terms, as quoted in Ingalls' *The Valley Road*: "...this area has dykes of igneous material extruded through the strata of sedimentary rock. The dykes are composed of ferrous material with relatively high power of heat conductivity." Dykes or dikes are defined in Webster's Collegiate Dictionary as, "a tabular body of igneous rock that has been injected while molten into a fissure, often resisting erosion and standing like a wall." When, eons ago, these dykes were thrust up and forced through the sedimentary rock strata, the strata were shattered and fractured. Then, when rain works it way down into the earth where it meets these fractures, it seeps along them until it comes to a dyke. There it is warmed and eventually resurfaces as a thermal spring.

The Warm Springs, now known as the Jefferson Pools, are located very near the juncture of Route 39 and Route 220, at the foot of Warm Springs Mountain. The men's bath house was constructed in 1761 and is no doubt one of the oldest spa

Ruins of the Bath Alum Springs bathing area.

structures still in existence. Adjacent to the men's pool is the women's bath house which was built in 1836. The waters of both pools are about 98 degrees Fahrenheit, and bathers can actually see and feel the spring bubbling under their feet. The pools have remained segregated, however, at designated times, both pools are open for family use.

For many years the Warm Springs enjoyed far more popularity than the Hot Springs. It was the place to be.

There was a huge hotel, the Warm Springs Hotel, which offered fine accommodations and a vibrant social scene. The common practice was to bathe in the pools for about 20 minutes, twice a day. One was instructed to be fairly still and quiet while in the water. Even today, there is usually a quiet reverence that is observed while bathing. The water is delightful and the experience blissful. One frequent visitor to the pools described her experiences as stepping back in time. She recalls that when she first went to 'take the waters' she felt a sense of calmness, and an overwhelming appreciation of the beauty of not only the water but also of the primitive structure that encloses the 60,000 gallons of water in the pool. "As I stood chest high in this warm, bubbly water and looked at the old chair that Mrs. Robert E.

The reflection of the ceiling of the women's pool looking through four feet of water.

The women's bath house built in 1836.

Lee used to be lowered into the water for her to 'take the cure,' I was overcome with a fascination and a love for the pool's history."

Today the pools are owned and operated by ClubResorts, the present owners of The Homestead. They are opened most of the year and anyone wanting to forget their troubles and escape the stresses of daily life should spend an hour in the Appalachian Leopard's "Spring of Strength."

The men's bath house built in 1761.

Five miles down the Warm Springs Valley the motorist comes into the little town of Hot Springs, which is dominated by one of the most beautiful and inviting hotels in America: The Homestead. There are many mineral hot springs on The Homestead grounds and these springs were at one time considered primarily useful for medicinal purposes. According to Fay Ingalls, "Experience of more than a century with these waters had developed a technique and a certain amount of equipment for their use." For example, shelters were built over many of the springs and the use of wooden pipes to direct the flow of the waters came into practice.

35

1899 ad from Harper's Magazine.

Originally, the many springs came out of the ground in a scattered fashion. Oddly enough, even though close to one another, they were all different in temperature, different in quantity of flow, and in mineral content. The largest of the springs was called the 'Boiler spring.' As its name indicates, it was hotter than the others. Today, several of the springs' waters are channeled together to provide The Homestead's swimming pool.

Although the various springs on The Homestead's grounds were said to have curative powers, they were not routinely used for drinking. It was the waters from the Healing Springs, about three miles south of The Homestead on Route 220, that were sought after for potability. Of the major health spas in the Warm Springs Valley, Healing Springs has remained the least developed. The temperature of the Healing Spring is about 84 degrees Fahrenheit and the mineral content is similar to the Hot springs but in differing proportions.

As the name "Healing Springs" indicates, these waters were thought to be powerful healing agents and they were bottled in large quantities and sold all over the country for several years. It was said that the waters were helpful in curing skin conditions, rheumatism, bronchial complaints, and in curing disorders of the urinary and digestive organs. The Healing Springs Hotel, built in the 1850s, is no longer in existance. Its replacement, the Cascades Inn, stands but is no longer in operation and is near the extraordinary Cascades Golf Course, considered the number one golf course in Virginia.

A treat for the feet at the outdoor hot springs on The Homestead grounds.

The swimming pool at The Homestead which is fed by the hot springs.

Healing Springs. From the Beers, F. W. Illustrated Atlas of City of Richmond, 1876. Library of Virginia.

Cascades Club. Circa 1895. Built by Jacob Rubino for his private residence. Just beyond the front entrance was a lavish swimming pool filled with Little Healing spring water. Rick and Becky Armstrong collection.

Rubino Healing Springs Water at "Little Healing." Bath County Historical Society

The Homestead

Among the great old resort hotels of the world, there may be a few that can be said to match The Homestead in beauty of setting, warmth of welcome, and splendor of accommodations. But anyone with a memory of a stay at Bath County's mountain spa will be quick to deny that it has a peer anywhere. And any guest with a feeling for our country's history will be fascinated by the story of The Homestead and Hot Springs.

Aerial view of The Homestead and Hot Springs taken in the fall of 2003. Each of the houses in the foreground are closely associated with The Homestead and are also steeped with history.

The Homestead as pictured by Beyer in 1857. Ilustration courtesy of and Copyright© 2003, The Homestead, LC, and used with permission.

"The Hot," as Hot Springs and The Homestead are often referred to, has a history that dates back to 1766. Much has been written about this wondrous place and the reader is urged to refer to the bibliography and to read the works of Stan Cohen, Hugh Gwin, The Bath County Bicentennial History, The Homestead's own historians, Oren Morton, Fay Ingalls, Marshall Fishwick and others. The author of this book has consulted these works, and has drawn upon the information and insights they offer, while adding her interpretations and personal observations to give the flavor of the remarkable history of this great hotel.

The story begins in 1756 when George Washington who, as commander of the Virginia Militia during the French and Indian War, named Thomas Bullett, a trained surveyor, as officer in charge of Fort Dinwiddie on the Jackson

River in Bath County. During his tour of duty Lieutenant Bullett became friends with Thomas and Andrew Lewis, fellow militia officers. The Lewis brothers were surveying land grants in the area and, on June 27, 1764, the three men obtained a land grant of 300 ares that included all seven of the mineral springs in what is today Hot Springs.

According to The Homestead's archival information, "As was common practice at the time, Bullett induced a number of Militia members under his command, together with their families, to homestead on his property at Hot Springs. Under his able direction the spring pools were improved, additional cabins constructed, and in fact a rustic, one story wooden lodge accommodating about fifteen guests was completed in 1766 - - and it is believed that he named it The Homestead, honoring the homesteaders who had settled here and were responsible for its construction and the operation of his new spa resort."

It was thus that The Homestead got its start, and today those original three hundred acres form the heart of The Homestead's three thousand acre resort. On November 21, 1766, Thomas Bullett became the sole owner, having signed a Deed of Partition with Thomas and Andrew Lewis. Today, the founding of The Homestead is celebrated on that date honoring Thomas Bullett, the homesteaders, and the Lewis brothers.

The visionary Bullett realized that the only way for The Homestead to grow and prosper would be to attract large

The snow covered boxwoods that form 1766 in the circle in front of The Homestead.

numbers of visitors to the spa. During this era the "thing to do" by spa-goers was to travel from one resort hotel to another, spending some time enjoying what each had to offer. Thus, to induce guests to leave another spa and make the trip to The Homestead, a new carriage road through the mountains to the hotel would be essential. At this point George Washington

A postcard of The Homestead. 1904.

again enters the history of The Homestead. Shortly after building his hotel, Bullett made a formal agreement with George Washington and others to begin what was called The Mountain Road Lottery. Washington became the manager of this lottery and according to John Hoover, historian for The Homestead, tickets bearing his printed signature still exist.

Apparently because of competition from the promotion of other lotteries in Virginia at this time The Mountain Road Lottery was not a success. However, by 1772, a petition signed by citizens from several counties was presented to the Virginia House of Burgesses, requesting the appropriation of public funds for the building of new roads in western Virginia. Although this petition did not bring immediate results, eventually roads were built with appropriated funds. The first road to Hot Springs, ran from the west of Staunton through Jennings Gap and across the Warm Springs Mountain.

Six years later, in 1778, Thomas Bullett died, leaving The Homestead to his older brother Cuthbert, a well-respected judge, who thereupon sold it. During the next sixty years it passed through various hands without any notable changes or improvements until 1832, when it was bought by Dr. Thomas Goode, a Virginia physician and, like Thomas Bullett, a man with a vision concerning the future promise of the resort. According to the present-day historians at The Homestead, he, like Thomas Bullett, "understood what The Homestead could become, and how to make it happen. He is credited with some of the greatest innovations and growth in The Homestead's history."

Dr. Goode introduced revolutionary forms of hydrotherapy, including the Spout Bath which is still in use today. In this treatment a jet of water 105 degrees Fahrenheit is aimed directly at any bodily location on the patient that is in need of relief from pain or tension.

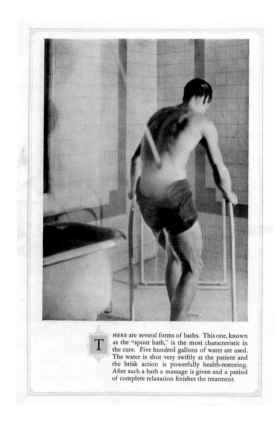

HERE are several forms of baths. This one, known as the "spout bath," is the most characteristic in the cure. Five hundred gallons of water are used. The water is shot very swiftly at the patient and the brisk action is powerfully health-restoring. After such a bath a massage is given and a period of complete relaxation finishes the treatment.

Reportedly Dr. Goode had three fundamental prescriptions for guests at The Homestead: taking the waters, enjoying exceptional cuisine, and experiencing romance. Under his ownership and management the hotel began razing and replacing the old buildings on the site and a new Homestead, three stories tall, and built of wood from the local mountains, was erected.

Dr. Goode ran The Homestead most successfully until his death in 1858, and left his mark on the resort that can still be seen and sensed today. His three prescriptions still apply to guests in the Twenty-first Century; their visits are synonymous with exquisite experiences in romance as defined as unforgettable adventures that engage the emotions as well as the mind and body. Some visitors come for the exceptional cuisine, together with superb service and living accommodations, to which can be added

The Homestead has been famous for both the most historic and most modern spa treatments for generations, as illustrated in this 1925 advertisement for its legendary Spout Bath. Illustration Courtesy of and Copyright© 2003, The Homestead, LC, and used with permission.

great golf and other summer and winter sports. But the third of Dr. Goode's prescriptions should not be forgotten: without the thermal mineral springs and the luxurious bathing experiences they afford, The Homestead most likely would never have existed.

A view of the back of the tower from the Breezeway connecting the hotel to the springs and pool.

The period following Dr. Goode's death, marked by The Civil War and the Reconstruction Era in the South, saw lean times for the resort. The Homestead was owned by a succession of absentee owners until 1888, when a spectacular change in its fortunes took place. In that year a group of financiers and wealthy industrialists, led by America's most prominent banker, J. Pierpont Morgan, formed a corporation to purchase the resort. Recognizing the extraordinary potential of the hotel not only as an investment but also as a significant contribution to the spirit of the times in late Nineteenth Century America, they determined to go further than merely returning it to its former glory.

It was during this era that the Chesapeake and Ohio Railroad made the valley more accessible by opening a line from Covington, Virginia, some twenty miles away. The route continued in use until 1970, when it became obsolete. But during its existence the C & O service to Hot Springs increased The Homestead's popularity and insured its continued existence despite fire, war, depression, and other vicissitudes.

J. P. Morgan is credited with transforming The Homestead into the grand resort it remains today. According to the Homestead historians, "Of all of the assets that the corporation and its successors brought to the Homestead, it was J. Pierpont Morgan's financial reputation, expertise, and the investment capital he could command that made the fastest, largest, and most lasting impact." Improvements included a new main Homestead Hotel, with an electrical power plant provided by Thomas Edison who was a regular guest. A new spa was completed with the most up to date hydrotherapy equipment. In 1892 golf came to The Homestead with the construction of the first six holes of the Old Course. Life was good, better than good, for The Homestead and for its guests.

This boom in development came to an abrupt halt on July 2, 1901, when The Homestead hotel was completely destroyed by fire. Fay Ingalls, whose family had been intimately involved in The Homestead's history and who served as president of The Homestead from 1922 through 1957, has written meaningfully about the fire in his book, *The Valley Road*. A youngster at the time, he remembers. "The roar of the flames was continuous but I felt rather than heard the noise. Ever so often there would come a crash or dull boom and a mass of flames would boil up, carrying burning sticks into the murk above. The hotel was only partially full but even at that it was a miracle that everyone got out uninjured. . .The next day I managed to get down to view the ruins, a great black hole with little specks of fire here and there and jutting up from this some chimneys and a few water pipes dripping senseless little trickles, where bathroom fixtures had hung. I...

Golf is The Homestead's favorite sport, and was colorful when the resort's club colors of bright red and white were 'de rigueur' back in 1920. Illustration courtesy of and copyright© The Homestead, LC, and used with permission.

came across a fine-looking old gentleman poking in the embers with a stick. When I tried to speak to him he turned away rather churlishly. Two or three days later I saw him again and he came up all smiles. I said something about his getting over the shock. He laughed and said, "Oh, That! It was nothing, and in these blue jeans and jumper over underclothes, I couldn't get a shirt, I'm really comfortable. But I lost my false teeth; I remembered throwing them out the window and, sure enough today I found them right under where my window was. Now, I'm all right."

Many of the grand old hotels that existed around the turn of the Twentieth Century were also destroyed by fire and were not reconstructed, but apparently the thought of leaving The Homestead in ashes was never considered. As the hotel was being rebuilt advertisements were circulated in major magazines and newspapers across the country telling of the progress and plans. One advertisement entitled 'Virginia Hot Springs; Magnificent New Hotel' read: " A New Hotel, magnificent in design and proportions and embracing every modern feature of a high class resort hotel, is being erected on the site of The Homestead at Virginia Hot Springs. All public rooms will be located on the first floor. The lobby will be 150 feet long by 60 feet wide and 20 feet high. Leading off from it will be a large

Left and right: Dinning and dancing at The Homestead in the mid 1900s. Illustrations courtesy of and copyright©The Homestead, LC, and used with permission. Center: 1950 menu. The Lyle collection.

octagon-shaped ball-room. Off the corridor leading to the dining room will be writing rooms for ladies and gentle-men. To the left of the lobby will be the offices, long-distance telephone, telegraph, elevators, ladies' billiard room and cafe, gentlemen's billiard room and cafe and the European cafe, as the new hotel will be conducted on both plans. On this floor, also, will be a large American plan dining room. The kitchens and entire working department will be detached and made absolutely fire proof. The hotel will be divided into several compartments by massive fire-walls extending through to the slate roof, with automatic fire doors in the corridors, on the order of divided

The amazing poinsettia tree of Christmas 2003.

compartments in great ocean liners, so that in case of fire in one section, that section only would be involved."

These types of ads were also letting people know that they could still come to enjoy the springs and golf links and that there were accommodations. The 1901 ad went on to read: "The Virginia Hotel and Cottages, affording ample accommodations for 150 guests are open, and, together with the bathing establishment will remain open throughout the winter." (Fred Sterry, Manager 1901)

"The Virginia Hotel and Cottages," also known as "The Virginia House," still exists. It was built around 1893 and,

The Virginia House, downtown Hot Springs.

because it had not only very attractive rooms, but also steam heat and plumbing, was a useful adjunct to the resort before the fire. After the fire it became even more important as a means of keeping The Homestead running during construction of the main hotel. However, with the opening of the all-new and improved Homestead in 1902, the Virginia House became less popular. The building was located next to the Hot Springs train station. It is said that when the train came and went to Hot Springs it belched much soot and smoke, that found their way into the guests' rooms. Today the building is used as rooms for The Homestead employees. It also has offices and shops on the ground floor, including The Homestead Market, featuring fresh bakery items, delicacies from the hotel's kitchens, and luxury food and wine.

The architectural wonder, The Homestead's Tower.

With J. Pierpont Morgan at the helm the hotel was rebuilt almost immediately. It opened for guests in March of 1902, only eight months after its complete destruction.

Special conveniences and amenities abounded with this newest rendering of the resort and there seemed no end to its progress and development stemming from the reconstruction phase. According to The Homestead, "The West Wing was opened in 1904, and immediately became the favorite of the entire Vanderbilt clan, who reserved many adjoining suites for their frequent visits. In 1914 the East Wing was completed and the Theatre, the Crystal Room and Empire Room and the Garden Room debuted in 1922. By the late 1920s additional space was again required, and The Tower was opened to much praise in 1929 - - and it has been our hallmark ever since." Indeed, when one thinks of The Homestead today, it is the hotel's graceful and elegant tower that comes to the mind's eye.

Dancing and dining at The Homestead

There is some irony that the tower - - The Homestead's triumphant and beautiful trademark - - was built in 1929, the year that marked the beginning of the Great Depression and nearly marked the end of the grand old hotel. The stock market crash and ensuing depression changed the course of history throughout the country and the world, and it is not surprising that a luxury hotel depending on affluent guests was deeply affected. Clientele and bookings dwindled and ten years later the Virginia Hot Springs Company, The Homestead's owner, was forced into bankruptcy. As a result the Chesapeake and Ohio Railroad, which originally had insured the hotel's popularity by making it more accessible, now became the holder of the largest investment in the resort. Somehow The Homestead managed to keep its lights burning during the 1930s, but times were not easy.

Just after Pearl Harbor and America's entry into World War II in December, 1941, The Homestead was dealt another blow when the United States government decided that Japanese diplomats were to be interned at the hotel for three months. Fay Ingalls, president of The Homestead at the time, remembers in *The Valley Road*, "... one day I received a telephone call from a Chesapeake and Ohio representative in Washington asking if The Homestead was prepared to make its facilities available for a war purpose involving the housing of five hundred persons who were going to be interned. The idea did not appeal but it was shortly explained that while this was a request from the State Department it was a wartime 'request or else.' The people we were to house were the Japanese internees, made up of the diplomatic and consular forces, representatives of the Japanese press, and some prominent businessmen. We were told that the treatment accorded these Japanese would determine how our people in similar straits in Japan would fare and our responsibility to help our own

unfortunates was stressed. . ..The Japanese were to receive the same service and same quality of food which was standard for other Homestead guests."

Downtown Hot Springs.

Agents of the F.B.I., one for every three of the five hundred internees, were on duty twenty-four hours a day so the hotel staff were kept very busy. The reimbursement that The Homestead received from the government was in no way sufficient to compensate for the costs of the added service, the loss of clientele, and the tensions that the internments brought to the resort and the community. There was a considerable sense of relief when the program came to an end just before the Easter holidays in 1942.

The Sam Snead restaurant in Hot Springs.

During World War II The Homestead was again called into service by our government. The United Nations Conference on Food and Agriculture, one of a number of international conferences to identify and examine the multitude of problems facing the peacetime world and to make decisions aimed at solving them, was held at The Homestead in 1943. The problems of feeding the starving populations throughout the postwar world could not have been more serious, and the decisions taken at The Homestead in 1943 could not have been more significant. Delegates came from every corner of the globe and, according to The Homestead, "We did our best to help them experience the peace that has been so much a part of our mountains and valleys for centuries, for that is our heritage of stewardship in this gentle place that is our home."

A view of the tower from the back-side of The Homestead.

It is no secret that the lives of Americans changed fundamentally during the postwar period from the late 1940s to the 1990s. People who in earlier times would have devoted themselves to seeking peace, leisure, and beauty became obsessed with business, making money, and obtaining possessions. The Homestead, always a microcosm of society, felt these changes profoundly. Loss of the regular, high society clientele of the old days, and failure to attract many guests from those dedicated to the new American lifestyle, brought The Homestead to a point of crisis. Financial difficulties prevented the resort from maintaining the high standards it had always set for itself. The spiritual ideas established by Thomas Goode so many years earlier - - his prescriptions of quality cuisine, romance, and healing mineral springs - - remained strong and true, but they failed to attract the new generation. More serious was the fact that the resort's infrastructure was showing its age. Regular guests began to wonder if The Homestead's doors would be open to welcome them for their next visit. Everyone close to the hotel - - staff, management, and Bath County citizens - - worried about what the future would bring.

Some of the charming wait-staff, most of whom are working their way through college. Left to right: Wanda Taylor, Pauline Eccleston, Shawn Peterkin and Verres Thomas.

At The Homestead it is said that time is measured in generations. This applies to the hotel's guests: generations of families have considered The Homestead as their home away from home, the highest compliment any hostelry could ask for. Not only generations of guests have considered the resort as their home but the same observation could be made concerning generations of the hotel staff. This is illustrated in Marshall Fishwick's *Springlore In Virginia* in which he recounts an interview with a Homestead employee. "What about the lives of workers? I talk with one: John Henry Folks, a spry twinkly man of 77 first employed here in 1916. Young John started on the golf links, moved to the hotel, and became printer in 1920. 'Some things can wait, but you have to have the menu every day - - that includes Thanksgiving and Christmas.' There was no assistant then, John worked only half a day on Sunday - - and set all type by hand until 1959. His father lived to be 96. 'My sister worked here, in the bath house,' Folks says, 'and my two brothers - one on the tennis courts, the other as steward. Later on my wife got on the payroll - - first as a maid, then in the front office. When our children grew up, 2 of the 3 got jobs at The Homestead. You might say, it was a family affair for us."

*Right:
Beautifully
potted plants
on a veranda at
the back of The
Homestead.*

Just when all seemed lost - - when people were reminiscing about the old times and the old connections and hoping against hope that things would work out for their beloved mountainous retreat, history repeated itself. An enterprise called ClubResorts visited The Homestead and fell in love with the somewhat dowdy old lady and recognized the possibilities for her future. ClubResorts purchased the Virginia Hot Springs Company/The Homestead in 1994 and, under the new owners' direction, has impeccably restored the failing infrastructure. What has been done is, in fact, restoration in the truest sense of the word.

*Afternoon tea
in the hotel
lobby.*

So, in a happy ending to our story, the old and the new generations can keep visiting and working at The Homestead, and Bath County still has its mountain spa attraction. Today when guests climb the front steps of the hotel's veranda and enter the main doors into the beautiful lobby, something happens. The gears that kept them running full tilt in the outside world suddenly shift and, along with feelings of awe at the beauty of the scene, a sense of comfort , serenity, and peace settles in. It is gratifying to report that The Homestead continues to represent hospitality at its finest. Every detail is attended to, and there does appear to be a destiny at work to insure that, as at every turning point in the hotel's 238-year history, the greatness of The Homestead will continue into the indefinite future. It will remain the noble and magical place it has always been, and generations of families will still be able to consider it their home away from home.

A monument on the Cascades Golf Course honoring Sam Snead. He was a renowned golfer who "amassed 185 tournament victories, more than any other player in the history of the P.G.A." Snead began working at The Homestead when he was 17 years of age and became the first golf professional at the Cascades Course.

Below: The Homestead. A view published in an undated pamphlet of the C&O Railroad. Library of Virginia.

Right: The Spa Gardens.

Above: The Homestead. Hot Springs from Porte Crayon, Virginia Illustrated. 1857. Library of Virginia.

Right: Cascades golf course club house and former home of Jacob Rubino.

Warm Springs

Warm Springs is as inviting and pleasurable as its name indicates. It is nestled at the foot of Warm Springs Mountain, just south of the intersection of Route 39 and Route 220. Over a century ago, a resident of the area said that Warm Springs: "...is a picture, soft and luxuriant, of rolling plains and rich woodlands, watered by crystal streams." The passing of so many years has changed little about Warm Springs; that description is still true today.

The Visitors Center on Route 220.

Aerial view of the northern side of Warm Springs showing the Jefferson Pools and The Warm Springs Inn.

The visiting motorist who drives into this charming community, is struck, first of all, by the exceptional care the citizenry has taken to maintain its character. Most of the buildings, whether official, commercial, or residential, have long and interesting histories.

So, you may ask, what happens in Warm Springs these days? As the county seat of Bath County it is the hub of the county's legal activity, with civil disputes, criminal matters, and property records all being handled here. And, as the site of Bath County's historic thermal springs, it attracts many tourists and visitors "taking the waters." Warm Springs may currently be on the threshold of development, but in 2004 it is still simply a charming little village that time and commerce have so far left unspoiled. Its population includes a mixture of retirees, people with second homes here, some who make their livelihood in the area's offices, schools, and businesses, and a few whose roots in the community go back for generations.

The men's pool. Circa 1761.

The women's pool. Circa 1836.

It is hard to generalize about Warm Springs because it is divided into three areas, each with its own distinct character and time-honored significance: first is the area bordering Route 220 on the east and west; second, to the west, is the old Germantown section; and third is the courthouse and its surroundings. Nearly every building in each of these areas is beautifully maintained and has its own unique history. The remainder of this chapter, with its illustrations and captions, will seek to do justice to Warm Springs as it is today and to some of the wonderful reminders of a bygone era.

The Warm Springs pools were recently renamed the 'Jefferson Pools' by their owners, ClubResorts, in honor of our third president who was a frequent visitor to the springs. The spa buildings are the first structures one sees when driving into Warm Springs from the north or east. There are two rustic board and batten buildings: the one covering the men's pool was erected in 1761, and the one covering the women's pool dates from 1838.

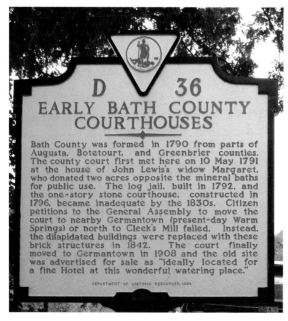

Both spas have remained virtually unchanged over the decades except for normal repairs and upkeep. Primitive and true to their origins, these pool houses are immaculately kept and offer bathers a pleasurable experience of stepping back in time to "take the waters."

Across Route 220 from the pools is the Warm Springs Inn, a welcoming hostelry and restaurant with an

impressive history. The core brick structure of today's inn dates from around 1843, when it served as Bath County's first courthouse and jail. In 1907 a new courthouse and county jail were built nearby in an area of Warm Springs once known as Germantown. After these moves, part of the old courthouse building was used as a general store, and the jail portion was remodeled to accommodate visitors of the Warm Spring pools. Guests at the inn today can still see where prisoners were held in the Nineteenth Century and dine in the old courtroom and judge's chambers.

Aerial view of the Warm Springs Inn and the intersection of Routes 220 and 39.

During and before the first quarter of the Twentieth Century spa-goers had several choices of places to stay in Warm Springs, including the remodeled inn and the luxurious Warm Springs Hotel, which was razed in 1925. The warm springs were usually the first place visited on the 'springs tour' and for many years far surpassed in popularity the hot springs at The Homestead. According

Idle hands of prisoners carved these images on the door of their cell in the latter part of the 1800s. This door is on display at the Warm Springs Inn.

to Perceval Reniers, author of *The Springs Of Virginia*, "...the fountains most strongly impregnated with minerals, heat, fashion and fame were the Warm, the Hot, the White Sulphur, the Sweet, the Salt Sulphur and the Red Sulphur." And the Warm were on the top of travelers' itineraries, not only because of their superior quality, but also because of their geographic location: the first turnpike into the area was laid atop Warm Springs Mountain and brought visitors directly to the pools. Moreover, the 'Warm' was also usually visited on the travelers' return trip, which added to its popularity.

Motorists continuing south on Route 220 will see a huge barn complex, an impressive group of buildings now in somewhat dilapidated condition. This is what remains of The Homestead's Dairy farm, which in earlier days produced much of the food for the hotel and its restaurants. In addition to dairy farming the barns and their surroundings were the site of extensive animal husbandry, with beef cattle, swine, sheep, and poultry all being raised

there. It is said that traffic on Route 220 had to be stopped twice a day to bring the Holsteins and Jerseys in from the pastures across the way to be milked.

The future of the dairy barn and farm site is now the responsibility of Celebration Associates, the parent corporation in charge of an ongoing project called The Homestead Preserve.

The Homestead's old dairy barn located on the east side of Route 220.

The project, which will be discussed in detail in the last chapter, includes significant plans for the old dairy. According to Charles Adams, managing partner of Celebration Associates, the site will be one of the first parcels to be developed. When renovated the dairy will become a community center serving not only Homestead Preserve property owners, but all of the residents of the county as well.

A little further down Route 220 one comes to the entrance to "Three Hills", originally the estate of best-selling author Mary Johnston. Her most famous novel, "To Have And To Hold," an historical romance set in Jamestown, Virginia, during the early days of English settlement, was published in 1900 and was enormously popular. Its success enabled her to build an estate high on a hilltop with commanding views of the Warm Springs valley and the "three hills" beyond. A place with an unmistakable mystique, the estate now serves as an inn where memorabilia of Mary Johnston are on proud display.

A snowy photograph of the Three Hills Inn.

A right turn off of Route 220, just beyond the visitors center, takes one down to a part of Warm Springs that was known as Germantown until World War I. Many of the structures in this area are quite old, and have been lovingly restored.

A notable restoration is Gristmill Square, a Virginia Historic landmark. A small stream, Warm Springs Run, has powered a mill on this location since the late 1700s. The present mill building with its picturesque waterwheel was constructed in 1900 and was in operation until 1971. In the early 1970s, Philip and Cathy Hirsh

purchased the mill and adjacent buildings, converting them into the Waterwheel Restaurant, together with an art gallery, gift shops, and an inn serving a few overnight guests. In 1981, this small, charming complex called Gristmill Square, was bought by the McWilliams Family who converted the shops into additional accommodations for visitors to the valley. Presently, the McWilliams offer outstanding meals at the Waterwheel Restaurant and twenty guest rooms.

Near Gristmill Square is Old Germantown Road, preserving the forgotten name of the area as a whole. Here visitors can enjoy the hospitality of the Anderson Cottage, a bed and breakfast owned and operated by Jean Randolph Bruns. This inn has been in Jean Bruns' family since the 1870s. While sitting in a rocker on one of the Anderson Cottage's spacious porches a visitor can enjoy calling to mind its colorful history which is in sharp contrast to the peaceful, unspoiled atmosphere of the inn today. Around every corner of the Anderson Cottage one can feel the presence of the past. In the words of Jean Bruns, "the original four rooms of log served as a tavern in the 18th Century. A second four-room cottage was joined to the first by an open porch, now enclosed as the front hall. A two-story brick kitchen dates from the 1820s. The property has been a tavern, ordinary, doctor's residence, girls' school, summer inn, family vacation home, and private home."

A short drive from the Anderson Cottage takes the

The mill wheel outside the Waterwheel Restaurant.

motorist to Warm Springs' third significant area - - what some might consider "downtown Warm Springs." This is Courthouse Square, which encompasses the courthouse and jail and other Bath County offices, together with the public library, the Bath County Historical Society and Museum, several attorneys' and other offices and private homes. The imposing courthouse, with its statue of a Confederate soldier on its front lawn, was built in 1912 after its predecessor, built on the same location in 1907, burned to the ground.

Jean Randolph Bruns, third generation owner of The Anderson Cottage.

Across the street from the courthouse is the Bath County Library, which is housed in the old Warm Springs Bank building. This important asset to the county's cultural life, currently run by librarians Sharon Lindsay and Jeannette Robinson, is the only branch of The Rockbridge Regional Library that is not in Rockbridge County. The library originally opened in 1973 in the old railroad station in downtown Hot Springs with Samuel Hileman as its first paid librarian. It moved to its present location in 1979. The library offers enriching programs for both adults and children, access to the 'world wide web', and an inviting meeting place for community groups.

A beautifully appointed room at the Anderson Cottage.

Finally, adjacent to the courthouse and across the street from the library, is Bath County's Historical Society and Museum. It may seem redundant to say that this museum is a treasure since all museums consist of holdings of treasured artifacts of our past, but this museum is something special. Its curator and keeper is Margo Oxendine, a well-known author and journalist who is currently a regular columnist for *Cooperative Living* and the *Alleghany Highlander.* The log and board building housing the Museum and Historical Society headquarters is itself a historical

A monument located on the courthouse lawn in memory of the Confederate soldiers.

The Bath County Courthouse. This courthouse was built in 1912 to replace the one which burned in the same year.

treasure, having once served as a lawyer's office at another location before being moved. The museum's collection of official records, books, incunabula, and artifacts is so complete that visitors can glean a true sense of Bath County's origins, history, and most of all, its people. With Margo's enthusiastic and knowledgeable assistance, one can dive into the archives and be held mesmerized for a long, long time.

To see more of Warm Springs, and to learn

The Bath County Library. The library originally began in 1973 and was housed in the old train station in Hot Springs. It moved to its present location in 1979. This building used to be the Warm Springs Bank.

more about this unique community, one can follow a self-guided walking tour, written by Jean Bruns, which is available from the visitors center on Route 220. A leisurely stroll through the village and a quiet soak in the Jefferson Pools will be a highlight of one's visit to the valley.

The Bath County Historical Society and Museum.

From Left to right: The clock atop the courthouse. The Warm Springs Market. The Warm Springs Inn.

Above: A barn on the Oakley Farm in Warm Springs. The house in the background was built around 1834 and the farm is a perfect reminder of how things used to be in Warm Springs

At left, Warm Springs Run.

The Library Cottage owned by the Von Schillings.

Christ Church located on Route 39 near its intersection with Route 220. It was originally built in 1852 as an Episcopal Church for Warm Springs. It has been beautifully restored by its owners and is now a private home.

The Warm Springs Cemetary located on Route 220 next to the old dairy barn. A walk through this peaceful spot will reveal the familiar names of so many that were once the heart and soul of this area.

HORSE PLAY

Horses have always been an integral part of humans' lives. Even during the time of this country's development, when the horse was the main means of transportation and when much labor was carried out by horse power, it seems that horses were also a significant source of pleasure and sport. The horse's status has changed in the machine age and it is now almost solely enjoyed in forms of recreational activities. Having done its job in helping to settle Bath County, the horse is now mostly used for pleasure riding, horseshowing, carriage driving, and fox hunting.

Etching of traveler paying toll from J. G. Pangborn, "Picturesque B. and O., Bath County Historical Society.

Melvin Poe leading the Bath County Hunt one foggy morning in September 2003.

The words 'fox hunting' are so evocative of the cry of hounds on a chase or the sound of the huntsman's horn calling in the pack. The very words conjure up images of 'pink' coats or thoroughbreds arching and folding perfectly over a panel fence. Added to these images are visions of the breathtaking hunting terrain with its open fields, rivers, and wooded lands. Probably one does not think of mountainous Bath County as an ideal place for fox hunting but the truth is that folks have been fox hunting in Bath since the late 1800s.

A social occasion at Fassifern Farm in the late 1800s. Bath County Historical Society.

A 1914 hunt scene at Fassifern Farm. Johnson collection.

Tate Sterrett was the first to organize a hunt in Bath County, at Fassifern Farm on the Jackson River. A hundred years previously, Fassifern Farm, which is situated about five miles from Warm Springs, was the location of the office of the first County Clerk, Charles Cameron, in 1791. In Sterrett's day, however, Fassifern was a much-loved summer retreat and it was there that he kept a pack of hounds and organized the Fassifern Hunt Club. According to Winants book, *Fox Hunting With Melvin Poe:* "Carriages brought spectators and participants to Fassifern from The Homestead for an annual horse show and race meet. The climax of the day was a point-to-point in which entrants dashed across the Jackson River."

Split rail fence as seen early one September morning on the Ohrstrom Farm.

The next milestone event occurred in 1932, when Rachel Ingalls, whose husband was the president of The Homestead for many years, founded the Bath County Hunt. Fassifern Farm remained the host for the hunt meets, but the terrain hunted was expanded, comprising a total area of seventeen by five miles and including neighboring properties. Fay Ingalls writes in his *The Valley Road* that: "The hunt was Rachel's personal venture and only because of her enthusiasm and hard work was success attained in the face of the obvious difficulties of fox hunting in the mountains." At its peak, the hunt met there three times a week with ten to twenty participants except when joint hunts were held and the numbers would go up.

Hunting activities ceased at Fassifern during and after World War II for a long period of time, during which The Homestead became the center of horse-related activities. It was the host for the Bath County National Horse Show and for competitive trail rides. And it wasn't until 1992 that the current owner of Fassifern Farm, George Ohrstrom, revived fox hunting in Bath County. John Coles, the real estate and farm manager for Ohrstrom, introduced him

to Melvin and Peggy Poe. Melvin, the legendary fox hunter of Orange, Virginia, was at a point in his life when he loved the idea of bringing his hounds down to Bath County and starting up the hunt again. Ohrstrom shared his ideas with Mr. and Mrs. Philip Hirsh, who owed an adjoining tract of land. The Hirsh's granted hunting privileges on their land, thus broadening the hunting territory.

Melvin Poe's hounds waiting for their cues.

From left to right: Joe Allen Conner, Clydetta Talbot, Katherine Conner.

Ring Master, Clarence (Honey) Craven of New York City.

As a result of all these efforts, together with the beauty of the valleys of the Alleghenies in Bath and, in Winant's words, "the charisma, charm and enthusiasm of Melvin and Peggy Poe," the newly-revived Bath County

Hunt has been a success. Considering the woes of urban living and suburban development, perhaps it is not so surprising that loyal followers are drawn from Northern Virginia, Albemarle County, Augusta County, and Rockbridge County, to hunt several times a week during each hunting season. The pictures on the previous page and this page

Conformation champion 'Cap and Gown', owner Gene Cunningham of Warrenton, Va., Mrs. J. Deane Rucker of Michigan, and Andrew Montgomery of Virginia. 1963

Betty Reynolds and 'Navy Commander', champion Working Hunter. The presenter is Mrs. T. Kenneth Ellis, Bath County Horse Show president. 1963

Left: Amateur Owner champion Mrs. Robert Motch on 'Isglide', of Keswick, Virginia.

Anne Mish of Lexington, Virginia and 'Crescent'. 1963

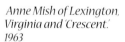

Phyllis Jones of Small Wood Farm, Crozet, Virginia, leads the way in The Homestead's fifty-mile endurance trail ride. 1965

75

with the exception of the one of Phyllis Jones are from the "Homestead Spectator," 1963. Photograph Copyright The Homestead, Hot Springs, Virginia 24445; used with permission.

Mrs. Fay Ingalls riding side saddle. She was an inspiration to horse-people everywhere and was instrumental in beginning and keeping alive the horse sport in Bath County

Amateur Owner champion Mrs. J. L. Lloyd of Oakton, Virginia, receives the fruits of victory from Mrs. Fay Ingalls of Hot Springs.

BACOVA

There are not many little communities in Virginia more charming than Bacova, which is located west of Warm Springs, one mile off Route 39. The village owes its name to Clarence M. Hudson, head of the Tidewater Hardwood Company which was in charge of nearly everything going on there in the 1920s. Mr. Hudson, obviously a pioneer in devising acronyms, took the first two letters of the two words "Bath" and "County" and the abbreviation of "Virginia" and came up with BACOVA to designate his company's town.

View coming into Bacova off Route 39.

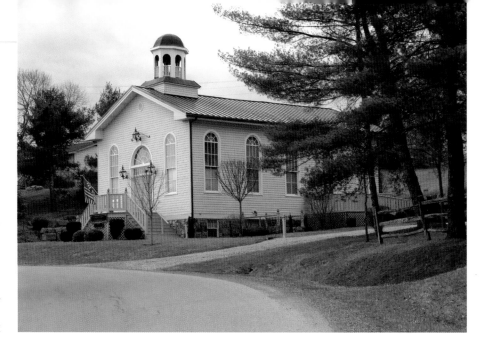

The town was officially established in 1920 by the Tidewater Hardwood Company. Within two years Bacova had a state-of-the-art lumber mill and the town developed around the mill. As recounted by Elizabeth McClung: "By 1922 there was a small office building, a commissary building, a church, a row of eight two-story houses for executives, and 42 cottages set in a semi-circular pattern around a small park."

The former Bacova Chapel which is now an art gallery.

Logs came to the mill from surrounding counties on two narrow-gauge railroads, and hikers in the western Virginia woods can still find spikes and other souvenirs on the ancient rights-of-way. Once there the logs were dumped into a large pond where they soaked for up to two weeks. Then they were sawed and loaded back on the rail cars to be shipped out. According to McClung: "At its peak in the late 1920s, the mill at Bacova had as much as 19 million board feet of hardwood lumber stacked on its south side. In a normal 10-hour day 100,000 board feet could be sawed." It was said to be the largest lumber operation on the east coast.

By all accounts Bacova in the 1920s was the perfect example of a company town. The little village was apparently quite self-sufficient. Day to day living was a communal effort, with tasks such as raising food being shared by everyone. The Tidewater Hardwood Company provided all necessities for its employees. The employees were paid in scrip which was used for rent, doctors' fees, supplies from the company store, and other needs. Bacova had the first water and sewage systems in the county. And, as McClung

The art gallery's sign.

The Tidewater Hardwood Company. Mid 1920s. Bath County Historical Society.

pointed out, "electrical power was generated by steam in the Bacova Mill's power plant. The lights were turned off at 8 am and on at 4 pm, with electricity left on through the day on Mondays so laundry could be done."

The village's first heyday did not last long. After ten years the mill ceased operation in 1931, leaving the town fighting for its existence and the residents who managed to remain extremely vulnerable. Whatever the cause - - the overcutting of the forests, the Great Depression, or a combination of factors - - Bacova encountered hard times until the 1950s. The town was sold to three private investors in the 1940s, but nothing happened to save Bacova from further decline.

However, a dramatic change in Bacova's fortunes occurred in 1957, when Malcolm Hirsh, a northern business-

The present home for MicroPhase Coatings, Inc.

man with family ties and personal roots to the county, bought the town outright with everything in it. How often do you hear of an entire town being bought or sold by an individual? Bacova had a moment of nationwide fame when Malcolm Hirsh appeared as a contestant on the television game show, 'To Tell The Truth,' in which the panel's job was to identify the "truth" the contestant was trying to conceal. Malcolm Hirsh's truth? That he was the owner of an entire town.

Hirsh wanted to fix up the town's infrastructure and then try to entice some new industries to the area. When no industries

THE BACOVA GUILD, LTD.
ON THIS SPOT... THE TOWN OF BACOVA WAS DEVELOPED, TAKING ITS NAME FROM BATH COUNTY, VA. IT WAS BUILT BY THE TIDE-WATER OIL COMPANY IN THE 1920'S. THE TOWN WAS RENOVATED IN THE LATE 1960'S AND THE OLD COMMISSARY BUILDING BECAME THE HEADQUARTERS OF THE BACOVA GUILD, LTD.

came, he founded one on his own, The Bacova Guild, Ltd. The Guild began producing laminated fiberglass gift items such as ice buckets, card tables, and the classic Guild item of the day, the Bacova mailbox. The durable and attractive fiberglass item, which has improved the looks of many a rural mail route, proved extremely popular. It was featured, along with other Bacova products, in nationwide gift catalogs and retail outlets throughout the country.

As small as this industry was, the Bacova Guild not only put the town on the national map but also, and more important, it put life back into the town. Hirsh sold out in 1981 to Patrick Haynes and Benjamin Johns. These new owners enlarged the operation and continued running the Guild for fifteen years until they sold it in 1996 to Burlington Industries. Once in Burlington's hands the Guild, as locals knew it, for the most part ceased to exist. The buildings of the Guild have maintained their identity but have changed hands several times. They are currently owned by Ken Wisehart and home to MicroPhase Coatings, Inc. which produces high-tech coatings. According to Player Haynes and Hannah Robertson, two enterprising youths who put out the "Bacova Bulletin," there are seven different coatings for industrial use being made at MicroPhase. One such coating keeps barnacles off the bottoms of boats and ships without affecting the water quality. MicroPhase has thirteen employees, with intentions of increasing that number to twenty or thirty by the end of 2004.

Today Bacova is a unique little mountain village and is well worth a detour from the more traveled routes in Bath County. Those forty-two houses set in a semi-circular pattern are now all privately owned. There still exists a 'common ground' that is owned and taken care of by all of Bacova's sixty some residents who make up 'Bacova United,' a cooperative created for the purpose by Malcolm Hirsh.

The welcoming sign seen entering the village of Bacova from Route 687.

An old barrel stave mill in Bacova. There is uncertainty as to whether barrel staves were ever produced here. Nonetheless, it is a handsome landmark.

A lone rider seen in the fog not too far from Bacova.

Lake Moomaw

One of the most remarkable physical features in Virginia can be found in the western part of Bath County: the Gathright Dam on the Jackson River, together with Lake Moomaw, the immense man-made lake that the dam created. Before the controversial project finally brought the dam and lake into existence there had been frequent

Lake Moomaw as seen from Route 600.

floods and degradation of water quality in the areas of the Jackson and James Rivers. The primary purpose of the dam was to bring the Jackson under control and thereby to prevent property losses and human suffering that had been all too common in the years before the project was completed in 1981.

According to the U. S. Army Corps of Engineers, "the dam controls a 345-square mile drainage area for the purpose of providing reduced flood stages at industrial, commercial, and residential properties on the Jackson and James Rivers." In addition, as the Corps has noted, the dam provides increased water flow during periods of drought. But for many residents of Bath and surrounding counties, the project's main accomplishment lies in the wide variety of outdoor recreational activities offered by the lake and its adjacent wildlife management area.

Originally the dam and lake were called "The Gathright Reservoir" and under that name the project was authorized by the United States Congress in the Flood Control Act of 1946. There is some irony in the fact that T. M. Gathright, Sr., whose name was finally attached to the dam, was opposed to the whole project. As Hugh Gwin has explained, Gathright "was owner of the property in 1946, and was not anxious to part with the land he had turned into a wildlife preserve." Gathright was joined in his opposition by various national and local Virginia environmental organizations, and the resulting controversy resulted in continuously delaying the project over a long period of

Aerial view of the Gathright Dam and the Jackson River below the dam in the fall of 2003.

years. Initial construction was finally begun in 1967, nearly twenty years after the original congressional authorization, and the project did not go into high gear until 1970.

Again, in Hugh Gwin's words: "Throughout all the opposition one man remained steadfast in his conviction that the project would benefit the area and made trips to Washington seeking funding for the project. His work over a thirty-two year period won him the name 'Father of the Gathright Dam.'

Benjamin C. Moomaw." On hearing the name 'Lake Moomaw' some people have thought that it must have some American Indian connection, but in fact the lake was named in honor of its principal active proponent.

The statistics connected with the dam and the lake are impressive. The dam is 257 feet tall; its top is 1,300 feet long and 32 feet wide. The lake is twelve miles long, with shorelines of about 43 miles. The depth of the lake is normally about 80 feet, and its surface area at normal water levels is 2,630 acres. Much of the lake's shoreline is adjacent to the 13,428-acre T. M. Gathright Wildlife Management Area, which is managed by the Virginia Commission of Game and Inland Fisheries. According to the Army Corps of Engineers, "this area is devoted to the production and management of wildlife, especially wild turkey."

There are legitimate arguments, pro and con, as to whether the benefits flowing from the Gathright Dam and Lake Moomaw outweigh the environmental losses and personal disruptions that inevitably accompany a project

A quiet winter day at Bolar Flat Boat Launching and Picnic Area.

of this size. Nevertheless, a look at the aerial photographs of the mountain ridges that envelop Lake Moomaw show how much of the natural wilderness has been preserved in Bath County. Indeed, the photographs give a distinct sense of the wilderness areas that still exist, albeit in smaller and smaller numbers, in our country. These ridges of

Aerial view looking northward of the mountains and lake in the fall of 2003.

the Alleghenies are part of the Appalachian Mountains, which run all the way from the Gaspe Peninsula in Canada to the coastal plains of Alabama. These ridges, often referred to as the Allegheny Front, constitute a watershed, with the streams on the eastern slopes draining into the James River and thence into the Chesapeake Bay, and the streams on the western slopes eventually flowing into the Mississippi River.

Aerial view of Bolar Flat and mountains beyond.

Bath County Pumped Storage Station

Not far from the Gathright Dam and Lake Moomaw is another little-known but monumental engineering achievement: The Bath County Pumped Storage Station. Deep in the mountainous Alleghenies and nearly surrounded by the George Washington National Forest, this hydroelectric marvel is located at Mountain Grove, Virgin-

Aerial view of the early days of excavation of the project. Photograph provided by BARC.

View from the top of Little Mountain where the upper reservoir is located. The bare area four miles below is the lower reservoir.

ia, near the West Virginia border. According to the website of its co-owner, Dominion Power, it is "the world's most powerful pumped storage generating station" which "quietly balances the electricity needs of millions of homes and businesses across six states." In 1985, the year it went into operation, it was cited as one of the nation's most outstanding engineering achievements.

"The Rockbridge Report" published by Washington and Lee University explains how a pumped storage station

The lower reservoir. The low level of water indicates that water is being pumped to the upper reservoir.

works: "...by channeling water from a pair of man-made reservoirs through turbines, creating power. The turbines act as massive water wheels, forcing water through tunnels."

The Bath County station consists of two large reservoirs, with one higher than the other. The upper reservoir, which is actually located on top of a mountain, covers a surface area of 265 acres with a fluctuating water level of 105 feet. It is held by a dam consisting of 18 million cubic yards of earth and rock fill. The upper dam is 460 feet high and 2,200 feet long. The lower reservoir is larger but more shallow; it covers 555 acres of surface water with a fluctuating water level of sixty feet. The lower earth and rock filled dam is 135 feet high and 2,400 feet long.

Adjacent to the lower reservoir is a 20-story concrete building housing six 350,000 kilowatt turbine generators. Three huge tunnels, each over a mile and a half long and more than 28 feet in diameter, connect the reservoirs and the powerhouse. When electricity demands are low, water is pumped from the lower reservoir to the upper one. Then, when demands become high, as the Dominion website explains, 'valves permit water to run through the tunnels to the lower reservoir at a rate as high as 14.5 million gallons...per minute."

The dam at the southern end of the lower reservoir.

The eight years of work that went into this engineering wonder can truly take one's breath away. According to Dominion, "the earth and rock moved to construct the dams and other project facilities, if piled up, would create a mountain 1,000 feet high. Enough concrete was poured to build 200 miles of interstate highway." The project cost a total of 1.7 billion dollars and required a total of 32 million man hours of labor. Dominion's website notes that the station was built in cooperation with the U. S. Forest Service and that, "occupying a relatively small amount of land, it has had minimal adverse effects on the environment." The waters flowing in the two streams that were dammed

- - Back Creek and Little Back Creek - - are supplemented by storage from the reservoirs, improving drought conditions and enhancing the environment for fish and other aquatic life.

As the Dominion website also notes: The extreme fluctuation in water levels in the two reservoirs make them unsuitable for recreation. However, a separate 325-acre public recreation area containing two lakes [open on a seasonal basis] is located just downstream from the lower dam providing opportunities for fishing, non-power boating, picnicking, swimming, hiking, and camping.

According to Hugh Gwin, a noted historian in Bath County, "The project changed the heritage of Bath County in ways both obvious and subtle. Our people developed a new view of the world, and the world has come to know it in a way it was never known before. The Bath County Pumped Storage Station stands as a symbol of change and, with the revenue produced, a better future." These observations are borne out by conversations today with folks who worked on the project. It is obvious that many of them had never witnessed such a project. One woman, who worked in the mechanic shop, said. "When you went through the gates it was like entering another world. We, the people in this county, had never seen anything like it. They had a 'man-camp' outside the gate. It was no more than a place to sleep but many people stayed there during the week.' Another worker, a heavy equipment operator, recalls that when the project was completed, Senator John Warner stood before the thousands of workers and guests and said that it seemed that this massive project went like clockwork. All the worker could think of was the opposite. He knew that there were countless inspection

The picnic shelter at the recreation area.

problems and delays, not to mention several tragic fatal accidents and injuries. However, he was proud to be a part of such a massive project and grateful for the employment.

The beautifully landscaped recreation area located below the Pumped Storage Station.

Garth Newel Music Center

Travelers driving south on Route 220 from Warm Springs to Hot Springs will encounter some of the most glorious scenery in Virginia. Along the way they will also see signs directing them to "Garth Newel," the cultural crown jewel among Bath County's foremost attractions. Those who follow the signs will find a nationally-known

The entrance to Garth Newel.

The Manor House.

music center devoted to the best in chamber music and other forms of music of all kinds, played by virtuoso artists in a setting of peaceful, bucolic beauty.

"Garth Newel," meaning 'new home' or 'new hearth' in Welsh, is the name given to the 114-acre estate by Christine Herter Kendall and William Sergeant Kendall when they purchased the property in the early 1920s. Along with their interest in music and the arts, the Kendalls shared a love for Arabian horses, which they bred and for which they built an indoor riding ring near to the estate's historic manor house. Mr. Kendall died in 1938, leaving Mrs. Kendall to decide what best use might be made of her extraordinarily beautiful property.

The stable where the Kendall's Arabian horses were stalled is seen below.

Her initial decision was to donate much of the estate to the Girl Scouts of America, and that organization used it for summer camps for several years. This arrangement eventually failed to work out, and in 1969 ownership of the property reverted to Mrs. Kendall. It was then that she was introduced to the Di Ceccos: Luca Di Cecco, a cellist, and Arlene Di Cecco, a violinist, both gifted artists with the Rowe String Quartet in Charlotte, North Carolina. This meeting produced the idea of establishing a music center on Mrs. Kendall's property - - of uniting great music and an exceptional natural setting in the Allegheny Mountains of Virginia.

A bucolic scene from the Garth Newel property.

The Kendall's riding ring, which was later named 'Herter Hall' in honor of Christine Herter Kendall, turned out to have splendid acoustics, and the music center's first concert was given there in the summer of 1973. As quoted in the Bicentennial History of Bath County, Virginia, 1991: "Christine arranged for repairs to the buildings and created the Garth Newel Music Center Foundation with a board of directors to help support the artistic endeavors and make sure the property was taken care of." The Di Ceccos became the founding directors of Garth Newel, overseeing the administration and development of the Music Center and performing at hundreds of concerts over a span of more than twenty-five years until their retirement in 1999. Their contributions to the success of the Garth Newel Music Center cannot be overestimated, nor can the foresight and immense generosity of Mrs. Kendall, who died in June of 1981. As the 1991 Bath County History notes: "...though quite elderly...[she] was rejuvenated in spirit by her

Side view of the Manor House.

Herter Hall where the concerts are performed.

pleasure in the music which began to sound all around her. Her 90th birthday was an occasion celebrated by an audience and musicians alike during a Sunday afternoon concert in August of 1980."

There are many written testimonials from visitors who have experienced revitalization, inspiration, and peace of heart and mind at Garth Newel. "Taking the waters" has always been associated with Bath County's history, and "taking the music" at Garth Newel could be said to have the same healing effects as the springs. "Upon visiting the Garth Newel Music Center, for the first time, ...I opened the door quietly and was greeted with the loveliest, most peaceful sound I've ever heard. I took a deep breath and let it out slowly and began to let the music soothe my soul." (Quoted in *Bicentennial History of Bath County, Virginia*, 1991) In the words of Evelyn Grau, who has been with the music center since 1983 and is the artistic director and violist of Garth Newel, "...for many of us music is a universal language. May it ever speak to that which lies deep within each of us."

The Garth Newel Piano Quartet, consisting of Victor Asuncion, piano, Teresa Ling, violin, Evelyn Grau, viola, and Tobias Werner, cello, is the Music Center's resident ensemble. Jacob Yarrow is its Managing Director. As Mr. Yarrow has noted, "Our picturesque concert hall with superb acoustics allows us to perform chamber music as it was intended -- in an intimate and informal setting for small, friendly audiences..Where else can you enjoy a meal with musicians who just performed for you? Sip a glass of wine during a concert? Warm yourself by a crackling fire in the concert hall?" Speaking of the resident artists he adds, "Their concerts are informal, conversational, and even interactive. They have recorded two CDs and performed extensively throughout the United States and on five continents. In November 2004 they will make their debut at Carnegie Hall."

Caught at rehearsal. From left to right: Teresa Ling, violin; Evelyn Grau, viola; Victor Asuncion, piano; and Tobias Werner, cello.

Garth Newel has much to offer in addition to performances by the Quartet, individually and as an ensemble, and by numerous guest artists and groups. The Music Center provides first-class overnight accommodations, gourmet meals prepared by resident chef Ed McArdle, a cooking school, music holidays overseas, a summer music scholarship program for outstanding students, and an annual adult chamber music retreat. A statement of Garth

View looking up toward Herter Hall.

Newel's mission, expressing the commitment of all those responsible for the Music Center and its various activities, reads as follows: "The mission of Garth Newel is to share, explore and celebrate the infinite variety of chamber music in an intimate setting of natural beauty. This mission is nourished and sustained through high-quality performances, educational programs, and personal interaction among musicians and guests."

Mountains seen from the overlook above the Manor House.

The flower boxes on the side of Herter Hall.

Millboro and Millboro Springs

Nestled on a back-road near Mill Mountain on the eastern boundary of Bath County, the charming village of Millboro is today a perfect example of a quiet, peaceful, slow-paced Virginia town. From Millboro down a precipitous mountain road called the "Crooked Spur" is its sister community of Millboro Springs, located at the intersection

One of the many swinging bridges on the Cowpasture. This one is on the southern-most part of the river.

of two busy state highways, Routes 39 and 42. Together with their surrounding countryside, Millboro and Millboro Springs are home to about 1,500 people, including a number of retirees attracted by the area's beautiful scenery and quality of life.

Millboro has several churches, a small industrial park, a post office, a community swimming pool, and the Millboro Elementary School. The town also offers a general store and Sugar Hollow Creations, a gift shop featuring local country art and craft items.

The largest employer in the community is BARC, the acronym of the Bath, Allegheny, Rockbridge Electrical Cooperative. BARC was founded in 1938 as part of a nation-wide program aimed at bringing electricity to rural areas through the formation of cooperative organizations. BARC chose Millboro as its home base, partly because of its central location and partly because it then offered railroad service to bring the materials needed for electrification into the area.

BARC linemen in the early years. Photograph provided by BARC.

Today, BARC serves a very large area of Virginia and enjoys a high degree of customer satisfaction. The current manager and assistant manager, Bruce King and Clyde Hively, oversee approximately fifty employees. When asked what the future holds in the face of current trends toward deregulation and away from electrical cooperatives, Hively was optimistic. Together with its emphasis on personal service to its customers, BARC aims to continue improving electrical reliability and efficiency while simultaneously stabilizing rates.

Millboro Springs, Millboro's sister community 'down the spur,' boasts a store named "Millboro Mercantile & Grocery," an automobile repair garage, and a newly-opened restaurant named "Brookside." The eponymous "springs" are all now on private property and seem only a memory.

Present-day visitors to Millboro and Millboro Springs find it hard to believe that they once were bustling communities with strategic importance during the Civil War. According to Virginia Bell Dabney, Millboro was "...once a busy country town with trains coming and going, with four stores, four hotels (one claimed to have a hundred rooms), saloons, an undertaker, livery stables, and a millinery shop. By 1910 it had a bank and late in its heyday a Ford automobile dealership." A

A busy day at the Millboro train depot in the early 1900s. Hicklin collection.

*Cady's Tunnel.
Hicklin
collection.*

long time resident, Mrs. Harold Deitz, was quoted as saying that, "...in 1912 you could walk down the street in Millboro and find anything you needed. You didn't need to go anywhere else for anything."

Millboro's past is much like that of the town of Goshen, Virginia, just a few miles east in Rockbridge County. Both towns featured resort hotels and healing springs and were developed primarily because of the Virginia Central Railroad. In 1856 the railroad completed the tracks from Staunton, Virginia, to a small settlement, then known as Cabin Creek, and now as Millboro. To continue westward several tunnels had to be constructed through the mountains. The building of the first and longest tunnel, which was 1,335 feet long and is still in use today, was supervised by Henry Cady of New York, a construction engineer employed by the Virginia Central Railroad. People began calling the settlement around the construction site by the name "Cady's Tunnel."

The origin of the community's present name of Millboro is uncertain. In the late 1800s it was also referred to 'Millborough' as well as Cady's Tunnel. One can assume, like so many other Virginia locations with "Mill" in the name, a mill in the vicinity attracted customers to the "borough." Two other tunnels - - Lick Run Tunnel and Mason's Tunnel - - were being constructed at the same time. As more workers came into the area to work on these projects, an actual town with businesses and services began to take shape.

Richard Armstrong, a Bath County historian who has studied and written many books on the Civil War in western Virginia, sheds light on some significant happenings in the county. While there were no armed hostilities in the Millboro area, the Civil War certainly brought profound and interesting changes to the town and its citizens. The town, and particularly the railroad, became of crucial importance as suppliers to the divisions of the Confederate Army in the western part of the state.

As Armstrong states: "As a result of Millboro being a supply depot, various Quartermaster and Commissary officers were stationed at Millboro Depot. Some of these officers were: Captain William L. Powell, Captain Eli S. Tutwiler, Major James L. Corley, Captain Enoch M. Lowe, Captain John M. Orr, and Captain Thomas H. Tutwiler. The duties of these officers included purchasing rations for the troops, overseeing transportation for baggage, ordnance supplies, weapons, troops, and a number of other tasks."

Family posing along the railroad tracks in Millboro. Hicklin collection.

One incident is of particular interest because it involved the President of the Confederate

States, Jefferson Davis, and the Millboro Depot. At one point about fourteen rail cars were sitting idle because they were being used for storing supplies instead of finding their way out to the troops. In 1862 President Davis sent word to Captain Powell at the Millboro Depot that he needed those rail cars to be freed to transport troops. Apparently Powell ordered sheds to be built quickly to store the cars' contents so they could be put back in service as troop transports.

The dam on the Cowpasture River where Lowman's Mill used to be in operation.

To add to the town's importance during this time it was also the designated assembly point for conscripts into the Confederate Army in 1863. And in 1865 Millboro was occupied by General L. L. Lomax. He and his men were housed in shanties and in private homes as well as on public property. The Civil War must have been a tremendous drain on the folks in Millboro and they, like everyone else in the South, had much

Elsie Wood and company in Millboro in the 1920s. Hicklin collection.

recovery work ahead of them when the war ended. Nevertheless, Millboro apparently recovered quite nicely. The railroad tunnels were completed; tracks damaged by the Union were replaced; passenger service was restored; and

the Virginia Central Railroad became the Chesapeake And Ohio Railroad in 1867. According to Dabney: "The town was home to railroad workers and their families and to the people who provided services to farmers, lumbermen, salesmen, sawmill workers, and tourists."

This is a tank that was apparently brought to Millboro during WWI to guard Cady's Tunnel. Hicklin collection.

People actually made trips to Millboro for specific purposes. They came to "...have their horses shod, to buy clothing, furniture, coal, kerosene, lamps, lanterns, lumber, hardware, coffins and farm supplies," according to Dabney. The nearby Millboro Springs Hotel was host to guests from far and wide who came to 'take the waters.' It was the railroad that precipitated all of this growth in Millboro and not too many years later, it was the automobile that precipitated the eventual decline not only of the town itself but of the railroad as well. The train no longer stops in Millboro; the depot is only a memory.

Sugar Hollow Creations in Millboro.

In the mid 1990s, the publication of two books by Marge Reider, PhD. - - *Mission To Millboro* and its sequel, *Return To Millboro* - - caused quite a stir in the area. These books purport to tell the remarkable story of how fifteen people, mostly Californians, were found under hypnosis to have lived

The first offices of BARC were housed in what is now the Millboro General Store.

together in a previous life in the community of Millboro around the time of the Civil War. The books recount, in considerable circumstantial detail, the participants' recollections of life in Millboro some 150 years earlier, including references to Cady's Tunnel, the Bratton Family who were early settlers, the railroad, and even some underground rooms in the town of Millboro.

The books caused a minor sensation, and for a short time put sleepy little Millboro on the national map. It was the subject of stories on network news programs, received nation-wide attention on talk shows such as "The Phil Donohue Show," and was featured on a half-hour syndicated program concerning the occult and the unexplained. One review reads, "Read the two books completely, and you will be hard-pressed not to believe that some form of reincarnation exists."

Even today, after the furore has subsided and the books are largely forgotten, some Millboro residents still regard with wonderment the stories they tell and view their town as something special. Others dismiss the books as the product of mass delusions if not a hoax.

Kristen Campbell standing on the upstairs porch of the Millboro General store.

There are also residents who remember that there once was an institution of higher learning - - a women's college - - in the Millboro area. Research into the history of Bath County, has turned up little documentary history concerning

Millboro Springs College, including its exact dates of operation. Fortuitously, however, an annual catalog of the college for the school year 1906-1907, owned by Millboro resident Emmie Hicklin, provides tremendous insight into what the school was all about.

The Catalog is quite remarkable in itself. It contains about thirty pages with ten beautiful black and white photographs, each protected with a tissue fly sheet. Also of particular interest are several pages of water analysis including one analysis of Wallawhatoola alum water. The catalog states, "The waters are unsurpassed for purity and medicinal qualities, as the analysis shows. Their curative powers are shown notably in malaria, indigestion, all forms of skin diseases, nervous and bronchial troubles, etc. Dr. George C. Griffith, whose residence is on the college campus, will advise young ladies of weak constitution as to the use of the mineral waters."

Millboro Springs College Catalog. Hicklin collection.

Center and right: former faculty at Millboro Springs College

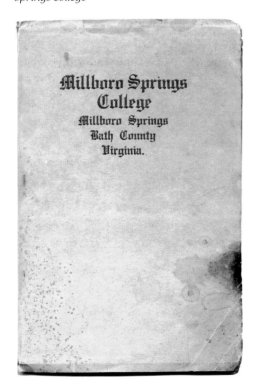

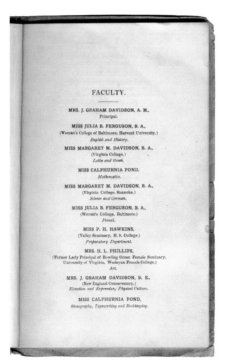

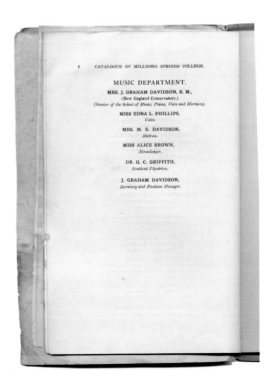

On the previous page are digital scans of pages in an original catalog from the Hicklin collection. The pages list the faculty, the courses they taught, and their impressive credentials. The curriculum too is quite broad and complete including studies of elocution, expression, and physical culture.

The Millboro Springs Hotel, which is now a restored private residence owned by the Lancaster family, provided the headquarters and campus for the college during the school year. A statement in the catalog signed by J. Graham Davidson, Principal and Business Manager, reads: "It will be noticed that the cost of living is relatively low. This is due to the fact that the school has the use of the property of the Millboro Springs Hotel, which during the summer months is operated as a summer resort. There is manifest economy in using this splendid plant as the boarding department of the college during the winter months, when it would otherwise be idle, and for this reason the college can furnish board at less than what it costs in institutions whose buildings cannot be made a source of revenue

This photograph shows the location and part of the Millboro Springs Hotel now owned privately by the Lancaster family.

Young women from Millboro Springs College going for a boat ride on the then Wallawhatoola River. 1901

during the vacation months."

Unlike other resort facilities in the area, the hotel/college did not perish in a fire, and one can only speculate as to why and when the school closed. But when we look at the building, grounds, and beautiful surroundings as they exist today, it is fun to imagine the bustling resort and college they must have been a century ago.

Young students preparing for various sports in front of the old Millboro Springs Hotel/ College. 1900

Aerial view of Millboro Springs at the intersection of Routes 39 and 42.

Millboro Springs Hotel/College. Lancaster collection.

Cows on the Cowpasture near Millboro Springs.

Summer Camps

In addition to the many day camps sponsored every summer by churches and other organizations throughout Bath County, the area around Millboro and Millboro Springs is the permanent home for three camps offering residential facilities and organized camping activities. The glorious countryside and its crystal-clear rivers and streams provide perfect settings for the camps and ideal conditions for achieving their aims.

Entrance to Mont Shenandoah off Route 42.

Mont Shenandoah's swimmng hole on the Cowpasture.

Camp Mont Shenandoah. As this camp's catalog says, "A beautiful setting, a wide variety of activities, long standing traditions, bountiful spirit and a family atmosphere have sustained Mont Shenandoah as a favorite camping choice for many summers." Describing the camp's setting as 'beautiful' is an understatement. Mont Shenandoah, located off Route 42, in Bath County, and bordering the Cowpasture River, is a magical place.

The camp is an immaculately groomed oasis in the forest where about 120 girls, ages seven to sixteen, are enrolled. Ann and Jay Batley are directors and owners of the camp. They are the third generation owners, and continue to instill the five virtues upon which the camp was originally founded in 1927. They are love, loyalty, friendship, sportsmanship, and spiritual awareness.

The dining hall at Mont Shenandoah.

It takes no more than a short visit to Mont Shenandoah to realize that the campers are thriving in their temporary home far removed from their accustomed cities and suburbs.

During the day they are kept busy with all types of sporting activities, including riding, swimming, archery, and canoeing. The camp also offers cooking, drama, and music lessons.

A soccer game in progress at Mont Shenandoah.

Ann is quoted in an article in "Cooperative Living" as saying, "These days it's about more than just having fun and making friends, it's a developmental experience for a lot of these young women and we're certain that the girls are happy campers while they are here."

Camp Accovac. Another camp in a beautiful setting in Bath County located just off Route 39 near the community of Millboro, is Camp Accovac. Occupying 84 acres bordering the George Washington National Forest along Mill Creek, Accovac is a non-profit Christian camp and retreat center owned and operated by the Virginia Advent Christian Conference. Hiking, biking, swimming, softball, and basketball are some of the popular sports the camp has to offer. The camp program is open to all youths of many denominations

Sign at the entrance of Camp Accovac

The area where Accovac is situated is rich with history. Once known as the community of Hotchkiss in the 1800s and early 1900s, it was home to a thriving sawmill called the

Millboro Lumber Company. Hard as it is to imagine today, in addition to the sawmill there existed a commissary, a chapel, and housing for the mill workers. And the Chesapeake and Ohio Railroad had a line that ran from the Millboro Depot to Hotchkiss that was used to move the lumber in and out of the saw mill as well as to carry passengers to Millboro and back for a day's shopping.

Old boarding house for the Millboro Lumber Company at Hotchkiss. Hicklin collection.

Below: a game of volley ball at Camp Accovac.

Camp Alkulana. Another Christian camp in the Millboro Springs area, Alkulana is located off the intersection of Route 39 and Route 42 on Lick Run. Originally intended as a camp for inner city children from Richmond, Virginia, today the camp facilities are available to both youth and adult groups, primarily those affiliated with the Richmond Baptist Association. Gracie Kirkpatrick, the camp's present director, says: "For all groups, we offer adventure activities that include tower rappelling, cave exploring, canoe trips, and low ropes courses and other initiatives."

The row of cabins where Alkulana campers stay.

At far left: Alkulana campers getting ready to swing.

At left: The popular ropes course at Camp Alkulana

Interestingly enough, Alkulana was begun in 1915 by the same woman who founded Camp Mont Shenandoah: Nannie West. Around the time of the First World War, Nannie West was the director of a neighborhood center run by the Woman's Missionary Union of Richmond, Virginia. She had a strong desire to benefit a group of inner city girls by giving them some time in the fresh air and peaceful scenery of the rural Virginia countryside. In 1915 she began taking them to Elmont, Virginia. Then, in 1917 she became a friend of J. Graham Davidson, owner of the Mill-boro Springs Hotel, and told him of her desire to bring her girls to the mountains for the summer. Mr. Davidson had an old mill on Lick Run that was idle and he offered that property for a camp. Eventually the Woman's Missionary Union purchased the property and it has developed into a ideal setting for the inner city children. The camp is full every summer and its success would certainly have made Nannie West proud.

Other Noteworthy Camps No Longer In Operation. There are many young adults, as well as middle-aged and older Virginians, who have fond memories of two other camps once operated on the Cowpasture River near

Nimrod Hall in the 1920s.

Left: Campers from long ago at Camp Nimrod for Girls

Far left: Nimrod Hall entrance sign off of Route 42.

Mont Shenandoah. One was Camp Wallawhatoola which was founded by Stanley Sutton and Dabney Lancaster in 1922. The camp ran until 1983 when it closed down. It was said that, "This operation epitomized the traditional image of a well-organized summer camp."

Nearby, at Nimrod Hall, were Camp Nimrod For Boys, which operated from 1935 until 1984, and Camp Nimrod For Girls which opened to campers in 1939 and closed in 1984. The founder and manager of the boy's camp was Frank Wood, and the girl's camp was founded and operated by Mattie Wood Poyser. Upon Mrs. Poyser's death in 1963, Frank Wood purchased the girl's camp property and his daughter, Sarah Wood Davis managed it until it closed. Sarah Davis, a leading and well-known figure in the county, now operates a riding center at nearby Vineyard Farm and has taught many youngsters in Bath County to ride.

Nimrod Hall owned by the Apistolis family.

Williamsville

Adventurous explorers of the highways and byways of northern Bath County near the Highland County border will be enchanted to discover Williamsville. This is a quaint little community on Indian Draft Road (Route 678) at the south end of the Bullpasture Gorge, well known among nature lovers for its dramatic beauty and profusion of wildlife. The gorge runs for some twelve scenic miles from McDowell in Highland County, ending at a bridge in Williamsville where the Bullpasture empties into the Cowpasture River flowing in from the northeast.

The abandoned Slim's Grocery in the center of Wiliamsville.

A parenthetical note about the names of these rivers is appropriate here. On first hearing of the Bullpasture, (fomerly known as Newfoundland Creek), the Cowpasture, (formerly known as Clover Creek or Wallawhatoola) and the Calfpasture, a river in neighboring counties, one is apt to think of grazing beef cattle. However, according to Oren Morton, the bottomland along these rivers was ideal grazing for buffalo herds; they are not animals who can live in the forest as deer and other like-creatures can. The Indians who hunted the areas actually were thought to have crudely maintained these river pastures for the great beasts. Morton further says, "The Valleys watered by the three streams came to be known as 'the pastures.' The names the rivers now bear were first applied to the valleys and not to the streams."

*The
Williamsville
Community
Center*

Although the confluence of rivers at Williamsville has been known to cause serious flooding at times, it is hard to imagine a community that is more calm and peaceful. The calming effects of the rippling waters of these rivers can be heard from many locations in the community. There is no hustle and bustle in Williamsville. It is a place where the few inhabitants all know one another and are a comfort for each other.

There are three times a year, however, when visitors from the outside world join the residents of Williamsville for celebrations and festivities. The first is in early spring, when Williamsville joins with the Highland County Sugar Maple Festival in providing unforgettable breakfasts in the Williamsville Community Center, cooked and served by

The Williamsville Presbyterian Church

community volunteers. The center is the only place outside neighboring Highland County where one can enjoy the traditional pancake breakfast with buckwheat or other pancakes, sausage, and maple syr-

Pastor Larry Brunson standing in the doorway through which at one time only men could enter. The women's entrance is on the right side of the church.

up made fresh from the sugar maples in Highland. One year the Williamsville Center sold about 3,000 tickets which translates into about 10, 000 pancakes!

Later in the summer, Williamsville comes alive at the joint annual Homecomings at Westminster Chapel and the Williamsville Presbyterian Church. Between them, these two reunions draw several hundred people, some local but many from far away. The Homecomings are celebrated with special music, good food, and boundless fellowship.

This same fellowship is celebrated on a third occasion in Williamsville at the Annual Lawn Party which is also held at the Williamsville Community Center. The event used to be held at the McClintic farm but the attendance grew so large it was moved to the Community Center. The Lawn Party raises funds to support the churches, the volunteer fire department, and other community endeavors.

At the heart of the these occasions is the Williamsville Presbyterian Church. In the words of local celebrity Donald Mc-Caig, a member of this church and author of several bestselling books including *Nop's Trials* and *Jacob's Ladder*, "This church is the center of the community. If not for the church, there would be no Williamsville." Pastor Larry Brunson has said, "The doors are open for all who come to worship. This is a fellowship of Christian believers."

The Westminster Chapel, sister church to the Williamsville Presbyterian Church.

The church has an impressive history and is one of the oldest churches in Bath County, second in age only to the Windy Cove Presbyterian Church near Millboro Springs. The present structure was dedicated in 1859 even though it actually first existed in 1784 as the Blue Spring Meeting House in nearby Highland County. During the Civil War, there were skirmishes and raids in Williamsville which are detailed in Armstrong's *Ambush At Williamsville*. As it is now, the church was also then the hub of activity. It was used as a guard house by General Mulroy's Union soldiers and even some of the villagers were held in the church during the occupation. Armstrong also says that the Union soldiers led "...their horses through one door of the church then up to the vestibule and down the other side to exit at the other door. Later, at the home of a Mrs. Byrd...who was devoutly committed to the church, they bragged that they had taken their horses to a prayer meeting."

Six miles southwest from Williamsville, at the junction of Routes 614 and 619, is the other northern Bath County community near the Highland County border. This is the village of Burnsville, famous among cave explorers as the home of many large caves. Bath County is home to over 100 caves, many of which are located and described by speleologists in *The Caves Of Virginia* by Henry H. Douglas. One of the largest Virginia caves, which is in Burnsville, is referred to as the Butler Cave-Sinking Creek System. Another very large cave is the Breathing Cave. Bobcat Cave,

A digitally contrived picture of the author's vision of a Union soldier and his horse in the church

which shares the same water drainage as the Butler System and Breathing Cave, is thought to be one of the deepest caves in Virginia, reaching depths of over 700 feet. Mr. Nevin Davis, a Burnsville resident and caver, was instrumental in beginning the Butler Cave Conservation Society, Inc. This is a nonstock, nonprofit corporation dedicated to the preservation, conservation, and study of caves. According to Mr. Davis these caves in Burnsville are privately owned and only experienced cavers can gain access to them.

A winding road near Westminster Chapel in the spring time.

Farm scence near Williamsville on Indian Draft Road.

The Bullpasture as it comes into Williamsville.

Trillium.

County Scenes

Windy Cove Presbyterian Church. Considered the mother church of all Presbyterian churches in Bath County is the county's oldest church. It is located on Route 39 in the Millboro Springs area. To the right is the church's cemetery.

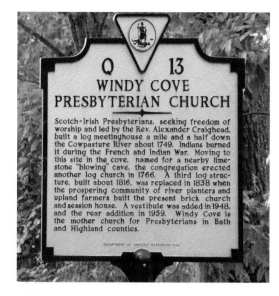

This building and silo constituting Fort Lewis Lodge is located on the property of Colonel Charles Lewis, one of Bath County's foremost citizens. The manor house (not shown) on this property was built by him in 1761. The present owners are Mr. and Mrs. John Cowden.

Left: This lovely pond as seen by air in the Mill Creek area.

Lower left: A farm scene in the Millboro Springs area near the Cowpasture.

Lower center: Rock Rest. Formerly the Bratton house and now owned by Emmie Hicklin.

Lower right: A barn seen on Route 600 near the Pumped Storage Station.

Aerial view of Healing Springs which is located along Route 220 South.

Aerial view of Healing Springs Elementary School.

*Aerial view of
Mitchelltown
along Route 220
South.*

Both of these pictures were taken at the overlook atop Warm Springs Mountain.

Bath County High School.

Ingalls Landing Field.

Log House located at Carlhoover on Route 220 South.

Sitlington Plantation. It is located near the Cowpasture in Millboro Springs and is one of the oldest surviving structures of Bath County. It was built around 1798 and is listed on the Virginia Landmarks Register of historic properties. It is privately owned by Mr. and Mrs. Robert Hilton.

Woodland Union Church organized around 1875. This church is located at McClung on Route 629.

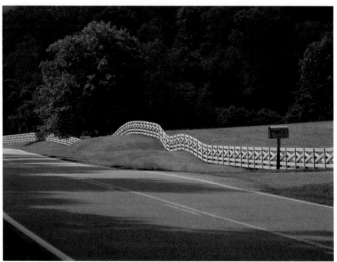

Route 39 in front of Bath Alum.

The steeple of Mountain Grove United Methodist Church.

The Gatewood House/Cash House. It is located in Mountain Grove on Route 600. Circa 1855.

Ellen Martin
hard at work
on the Cascades
waterfalls.

*Right: Windy
Cove Farm
owned by the
George Phillips
family.*

*Above right: Warwickton. Built
by Judge James Wood Warwick
in 1848. In 1992 Warwickton
and Hidden Valley provided the
location for "Sommersby," a Civil
War movie starring Richard
Gere and Jody Foster. It is now a
bed & breakfast operated by the
Stidhams.*

The Foreseeable Future

We have thus far seen that Bath County has managed to sustain its bucolic surroundings. Population and population density, relatively speaking, are quite low. The amount of protected forest land has and should in the future help to keep Bath the beautiful and uncluttered mountain and valley terrain it is today. However, change is inevitable and Bath will experience some transformations in the years ahead. One can hope that these changes

Aerial view of the golf course and the back of The Homestead.

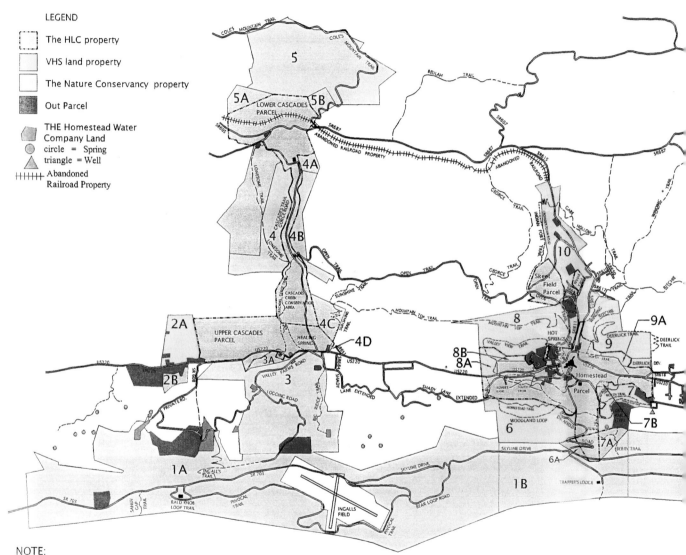

VIRGINIA HOT SPRINGS, INCORPORATED (VHS) / THE HOMESTEAD, L.C. (HLC)/ THE NATURE CON
PROPERTY MAP (PROPOSED) REVISED 9/12/02

This map is a general representation of the relationship of The Homestead Preserve to the valley. The portions in yellow are slated for development.

LEGEND

The HLC property

VHS land property

The Nature Conservancy property

Out Parcel

THE Homestead Water Company Land
circle = Spring
triangle = Well

Abandoned Railroad Property

NOTE:
This Property Map is intended to depict, in general terms, the ownership of the property shown hereon following the proposed conveyance of property between VHS and HLC. This
only as a conceptual depiction of the property boundaries, roads and other matters shown hereon, and this Property Map is not based on a land survey or other such precise inform
foregoing, there are known out parcels that previously have been conveyed out of the properties shown on this Property Map which are not depicted as out parcels hereon. The de
matters on this Property Map is not intended to, and shall not be construed to, constitute a dedication thereof for public use.
As used herein, "VHS" shall mean Virginia Hot Springs, Incorporated, "TNC" shall mean The Nature Conservancy and "HLC" shall mean The Homestead, L.C.

144

ANCY (TNC)

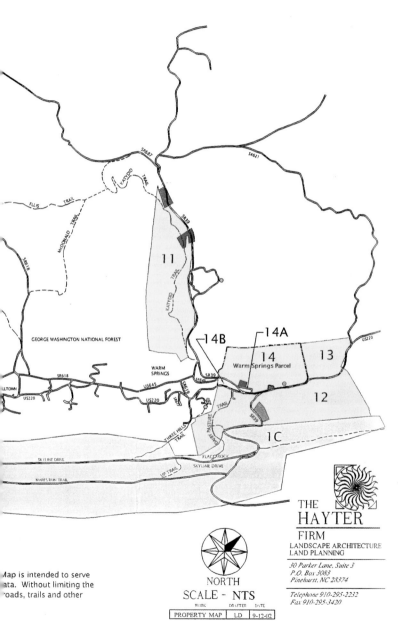

GEORGE WASHINGTON NATIONAL FOREST

14B 14A
14
Warm Springs Parcel
13

WARM SPRINGS

12

1C

THE
HAYTER
FIRM
LANDSCAPE ARCHITECTURE
LAND PLANNING

30 Parker Lane, Suite 3
P.O. Box 3083
Pinehurst, NC 28374

Telephone 910-295-2232
Fax 910-295-3420

Map is intended to serve
ata. Without limiting the
oads, trails and other

NORTH
SCALE - NTS

| WORK | DRAFTER | DATE |
| PROPERTY MAP | LD | 9-12-02 |

will be friendly both to the citizens of Bath and the geographical region itself.

The most dramatic change that is about to occur in Bath County is a project called The Homestead Preserve. This project is parented by Celebration Associates. Before giving a brief description of the development plans, a little background information will be not only interesting but will also be helpful in understanding how The Homestead Preserve came about and its relationship to The Homestead.

The Virginia Hot Springs, Inc., owned The Homestead and 15,000 acres surrounding it for much of The Homesteads history. However, in 1994 ClubResorts purchased The Homestead, the golf courses and 3,000 acres from the Virginia Hot Springs, Inc. ClubResorts is a subsidiary of ClubCorp, a Dallas based company. ClubResorts also owns The Pinehurst Resorts, a major golf resort in North Carolina and Barton Creek Resort and Spa in Austin, Texas. When this transaction occurred, the Virginia Hot Springs, Inc. retained 12,000 acres but gave ClubResorts an option to purchase the additional land at a later date.

ClubResorts declined to purchase the 12,000 acres but in March 2002, Celebration Associates, who had had business ties with ClubResorts in previous years, acquired 100% of the stock in the Virginia Hot Springs, Inc. and with that acquisition came the 12,000 acres. On the very day that the deal was sealed, 9,000 acres atop Warm Springs Mountain were turned over to The Nature Conservancy, a well-known environmental conservation organization. The remaining acreage owned by Celebration Associates is slated for development within the project called The Homestead Preserve.

According to Charles Adams, Celebration Associates managing partner, the project includes a maximum of 450 residential properties spread over approximately 2,300 acres with only 325 acres actually being disturbed by construction. It is estimated that most of these homes will be second or vacation homes ranging in price from $225,000 to $1,000,000. Adams further states that the buyers will be able to purchase memberships at The Homestead which will provide an attractive sales incentive for his company and an opportunity to enhance the golf and tennis business at The Homestead.

Dr. Don Messmer, of William and Mary College has been hired by Celebration Associates to conduct an economic impact study on the effects of this development project. Although his study will not be concluded before publication of this book, Dr. Messmer states: "Generally speaking, housing developments with homes costing in excess of $300,000 have a positive impact because the

The mountains as seen from Mountain Grove on Route 600.

owners are usually older adults who bring no children to the school system and demand few services from the local government."

The term "development" strikes fear in many of us. We long for our environs to stay unspoiled and we often resist change. The Homestead Preserve will bring changes to Bath County, some good and some not so good. There is no possibility of building 450 new homes without fundamentally affecting the county and its citizens. There will be a need for more of everything: more roads, more waste and sewage disposal, more businesses and public services, and many more challenges. There is one thing certain and that is that the Warm Springs Valley will be taking on a new look over the next ten years.

A farm scene on Mill Creek road.

Another fairly significant project will be the construction of a retirement home which will be located on the

hill behind the Bath County High School. In the mid-1990s, the Retirement Home Commission was formed to conduct a feasibility study for housing for the elderly in Bath County. After mailing out 3,000 surveys to Bath citizens and analyzing the returned questionnaires, it was apparent that such housing was needed. This housing project is headed by the Waynesboro Housing Authority and construction is to begin in the fall of

2004. The plans call for twenty-eight one and two bedroom apartments with a community center. It is hoped that the project will be completed in 2005 with full occupancy by early 2006.

In contrast to the development activity now taking place in the Warm Springs Valley, the pace of change in eastern Bath County promises to be slower. At the time of this writing there seem to be no significant plans for development in the near future. One can only speculate that there will be a slow but steady influx of retired persons wanting to get away from the trials and tribulations of city life. Eastern Bath County must expect to face the same problems faced by rural communities throughout the United States - - the continuing loss of family farms, the shrinking acreage devoted to agriculture and animal husbandry, the aging population, and the lack of career opportunities necessary to keep young people from leaving. But the people who live here truly love their part of the world. While welcoming new neighbors, they will be happy if the changes in their world take place gradually, without destroying something that is hard to define but that they recognize as irreplaceable.

A typical view of Bath County from the air.

The compelling force behind this book, was two-fold: to give a fresh look to a very old story that constitutes Bath's history, and to show the reader, through photographs from the ground and from the air, the Bath of today. In its own quiet way, the Bath of today is spectacular and it is up to those of us who care about its future to take inspiration from that fact and to do everything in our power to maintain its spectacular beauty and quality of life.

Dam on the Douthat State Park Lake.

Bibliography

Armstrong, Richard L., *The Civil War in Bath County, Virginia*, Hot Springs, Virginia, 1994.

Armstrong, Richard L., *Ambush At Williamsville*, Hot Springs, Virginia, 1986.

Bath County Historical Society, Warm Springs, Virginia.

Bath County Historical Society, *The Bicentennial History of Bath County, Virginia 1791-1991*, Heritage House Publishing, Marceline, Mo., 1991.

Cohen, Stan, *Historic Springs of The Virginias*, Pictorial Histories Publishing Co., Charleston, West Virginia, 1984.

Cohen, Stan, *The Homestead and Warm Springs Valley Virginia*, Pictorial Histories Publishing Co., Charlestown, West Virginia, 1981.

Cooperative Living, March/April 2003, "Beyond Bug Spray and Boy Talk," by Laura Hickey.

Dominion, http://www.dom.com

Douthat State Park, http//www.dcr.state.va.us/parks/douthat.htm

Douglas, Henry, H., *The Caves of Virginia*, Virginia Cave Survey, Falls Church, Virginia, 1964.

Fishwick, Marshall, *Springlore in Virginia*, Popular Press, Bowling Green State University, 1978.

Gwin, Hugh S., *Historically Speaking True Tales of Bath County, Virginia*, The Bath County Historical Society, Inc. Warm Springs, Virginia, 2001.

Haynes, Player, and Robertson, Hanna, *The Bacova Bulletin*, January 2004.

The Homestead Spectator, Hot Springs, Virginia, 1963.

The Homestead Spectator, Hot Springs, Virginia 1966.

Ingalls, Fay, *The Valley Road*, The World Publishing Company, New York, 1949.

McAllister, Jean Graham, *A Brief History of Bath County, Virginia*, McClure Printing, Staunton, Virginia 1920.

Millboro Springs College Catalog, Bath County, Virginia, 1906.

The Nature Conservancy, http://nature.org/success/warmsprings.html

The Recorder, Volume 127 No. 25, Bath and Highland County, June 2004.

Reniers, Perceval, *The Springs of Virginia*, University of North Carolina Press, 1941.

Reider, Marge, Ph.D., *Mission To Millboro*, Blue Dolphin Publishing, Inc., California, 1993.

Reider, Marge, Ph.D., *Return To Millboro*, Blue Dolphin Publishing, Inc., California, 1993.

Valley Conservation Council, *The State of the Valley*, 2003.

Virginia Historical Society, *Firsts Resorts: A Visit to Virginia's Springs*, Richmond, Virginia, 1987.

Winegar, Deane and Garvey, *Highroad Guide to the Virginia Mountains*, Longstreet Press, 1988.

Winants, Peter, *Fox Hunting With Melvin Poe*, The Derrydale Press, New York, 2002.